Suga

LO
SIGNS

SCORPIO

23 OCTOBER–22 NOVEMBER

by Jacqui Deevoy

Your heavenly guide to
LIFE, LOVE and BOYS

It's cosmic!

mustard

First published in 1999 by Mustard

Mustard is an imprint of Parragon

Parragon
Queen Street House
4 Queen Street
Bath BA1 1HE
UK

Produced by Magpie Books, an imprint of
Robinson Publishing Ltd, London

Page design by Sandie Boccacci

ISBN 1-84164-191-X

A copy of the British Library Cataloguing-in-Publication Data is available from the British Library

Printed and bound in the EC

Contents

Part 10: YOUR YEAR AHEAD: THE YEAR 2000 AT A GLANCE

Part 11: INTO THE NEW MILLENNIUM!

Part 12: BIRTHDAY CHART

For all my favourite Scorpians:

Mary-Ellen
Jonathan
Russell
Nova
Wendy
Eamonn
Liz
Rory
Sam

Part 1:

All About Scorpio

A Brief Introduction To Your Sign . . .

Scorpio is the eighth sign of the zodiac and is concerned with life, death, passion, change, secrets and magic. Ruled by the mysterious planet Pluto, you have a lot of hidden depths. It's Pluto you also have to thank for your magnetic personality and your love of all things weird and wonderful! Your best qualities are your compassionate nature, your inability to be shocked, your emotional side and your sensuality. But there's another, not so positive, side to your personality . . . You're sometimes accused of being self-destructive, moody, ruthless, sadistic and cunning. You can be, of course, but only when really pushed. You're very determined and when you have your mind or heart set on something, no one or nothing can distract you from going for it.

You were a serious child – old for your years, seriously competitive and very sure about what you wanted. You could be vengeful though, so woe betide anyone who played with your toys without your permission!

As a Scorpio, you traditionally get a lot of bad press. The truth is, it's only when you can't find an outlet for your energy and creativity that you start getting negative. OK, so you can be trouble, but you can also be rather gorgeous, in that you're sussed, sexy and kind. There! Feel better now?

You come across as very cool: you're very straight-talking, never beating about the bush when making a request. If you want something, you ask for it, then you get it: that's just the sort of girl you are! You find it hard to trust people who use flattery and compliments to get what they want, and because of this you can be generally fairly suspicious of anyone who appears to be "nice". You like to get out and about, but basically you love your own space and your family and would rather be at home than anywhere else in the world.

Although you can be a tad stand-offish, you actually have a deep need to be emotionally involved with others. Your biggest problem is the fact that you find it so hard to let people know this. In fact, you find it almost impossible to admit to – let alone discuss – any worries you might have. You believe your reluctance to offload your grievances is because you're such a strong person. And to a large degree that's true. But it's only when you finally learn to connect more intimately with others that you'll really find out what life is all about.

Here you are in a nutshell:

You're great . . . because you're intelligent, extremely attractive and have a wonderful air of mystery.

You grate . . . because you've got a massive jealous streak, you can be quite nasty if someone upsets you and you're unbearably nosy!

You rate ... all things weird and wonderful, getting to the bottom of a mystery and snogging (in abundance preferably!).

You hate ... being asked too many questions (strange for one so inquisitive), admitting ignorance and people who are cleverer than you.

You're late ... very rarely. If you are, it'll be for a good reason.

As a mate ... you're a laugh-a-minute type and treat your friends like family. But your need to know absolutely everything about your friends can sometimes be offputting for those who get involved with you.

As a date ... you're deep, honest but may find it hard to express your true feelings.

Your fate: To learn how to be open.

Lucky Stuff

Numbers: 9 for Scorpio *and* for Pluto, your ruling planet.

Day: Tuesday. (Well, *someone* has to like it!)

Colours: Dark red, rust and black.

Gemstones: Rubies and opals – both on the same ring preferably! (Don't ask for much, do you, Scorpio?!)

Metals: Iron and steel.

Flowers: Geraniums, heather and chrysanthemums. All very dramatic, beautiful and totally Scorpian. You also like cactii – dry and prickly, just the way you can be at times!

Food: Anything strong-tasting – onions are a particular fave. You also have a penchant for tomatoes or anything tomato-flavoured.

Animals: Wolf, lizard and panther – stealthy, cunning and kinda slinky! Just like you!

Birds: Eagle and vulture. Like a Scorpio, they never miss a trick.

Cities: Dover, Halifax, Liverpool, Newcastle, Stockport, New Orleans, Washington DC and Valencia. If you're a Scorpian living in one of these cities already, count yourself extra lucky!

Your Rising Sign = The You Others See

In astrology, if you want to discover more about your outer personality and how you come across to others, it helps if you know your Ascendant. Working it out can be a problem, but using the specially devised chart over the page, it couldn't be easier. So look yourself up . . .

A Bit About Rising Signs

Your Rising Sign is the main indicator of your outer personality (i.e. how others see you as opposed to how you view yourself) and also has a major bearing on the way you look and the impact you make on the opposite sex. When combined with your Sun Sign, you'll get an even more accurate picture.

It's important to take British Summer Time into account when working out your Rising Sign. This period varies from year to year but, to keep things simple, if you were born between March 16 and October 31 of any year, subtract one hour from your time of birth. If you were born between midnight and 1 a.m. during the Summer Time period, your birth hour will be 11 p.m. or 12 midnight on the previous day. If you're uncertain about your birth time, all you can do is read through all twelve descriptions on the following pages and see if you can spot yourself. It shouldn't be difficult.

Born abroad? Well, find out the time difference between the United Kingdom and your place of birth. If you were born in a country that is ahead of the UK time-wise, then subtract the number of hours' difference from your birth time; if you were born in a country that's behind the UK time-wise, then add that number of hours to your birth time.

How To Use The Rising Signs Chart

1. Locate your birth date in the first (left-hand) column on the chart on pages 8 and 9.

2. Find your birth hour along the top of the page. If you were born between hours, work it out to the nearest hour. For example, if you were born at 8.45 a.m., your birth hour is 9 a.m. If you were born at 6.20 p.m., your birth hour is 6 p.m. If you were born at exactly half past the hour, go to the next hour (i.e. being born at 4.30 a.m. would give you the birth hour of 5 a.m.) Don't forget to subtract an hour if you were born between March 16 and October 31.

3. At the point where the two columns meet, you'll find an astrological symbol. Look up this symbol in the Symbol Index on page 10 and find out what your Rising Sign is.

4. Then turn the page, find your Rising Sign and discover more about the way others – blokes included! – perceive you. **Note:** If the description doesn't sound like you, check the sign before and after. Because the chart is general, 100 per cent accuracy is impossible for everyone who uses it, and some people may, by the skin of their teeth, fall into the wrong category.

RISING SIGNS CHART

TIME ▶ / DATE ▼	1 AM	2 AM	3 AM	4 AM	5 AM	6 AM	7 AM	8 AM	9 AM	10 AM
Jan 1–16	♎	♏	♏	♏	♐	♐	♑	♑	♒	♓
Jan 17–Feb 21	♏	♏	♐	♐	♑	♑	♑	♒	♓	♈
Feb 22–Mar 29	♐	♑	♑	♒	♒	♓	♈	♉	♉	♊
Mar 30–Apr 29	♑	♒	♓	♓	♈	♉	♊	♊	♋	♋
Apr 30–May 19	♒	♓	♈	♈	♉	♊	♊	♋	♋	♌
May 20–Jun 8	♓	♈	♉	♊	♊	♋	♋	♌	♌	♌
Jun 9–24	♈	♉	♊	♊	♋	♋	♋	♌	♌	♍
Jun 25–Jul 17	♉	♊	♊	♋	♋	♌	♌	♌	♍	♍
Jul 18–Aug 14	♊	♊	♋	♋	♌	♌	♍	♍	♍	♎
Aug 15–Sep 19	♋	♋	♌	♌	♌	♍	♍	♎	♎	♎
Sep 20–Oct 29	♌	♌	♍	♍	♎	♎	♎	♏	♏	♐
Oct 30–Dec 8	♍	♍	♍	♎	♎	♏	♏	♏	♐	♐
Dec 9–31	♎	♎	♏	♏	♐	♐	♐	♑	♑	♒

11 AM	12 NOON	1 PM	2 PM	3 PM	4 PM	5 PM	6 PM	7 PM	8 PM	9 PM	10 PM	11 PM	12 M'NT
♓	♈	♉	♊	♊	♋	♋	♌	♌	♌	♍	♍	♎	♎
♈	♉	♊	♊	♋	♋	♌	♌	♍	♍	♎	♎	♎	♏
♊	♋	♋	♌	♌	♍	♍	♍	♎	♎	♎	♏	♏	♐
♋	♌	♌	♍	♍	♍	♎	♎	♏	♏	♏	♐	♐	♑
♌	♌	♍	♍	♎	♎	♎	♏	♏	♐	♐	♐	♑	♑
♍	♍	♍	♎	♎	♏	♏	♏	♐	♐	♑	♑	♒	♓
♍	♍	♎	♎	♏	♏	♏	♐	♐	♑	♑	♒	♒	♓
♎	♎	♎	♏	♏	♐	♐	♐	♑	♑	♒	♓	♈	♉
♎	♎	♏	♏	♐	♐	♑	♑	♒	♒	♓	♈	♉	♉
♏	♏	♐	♐	♐	♑	♑	♒	♓	♈	♉	♉	♊	♊
♐	♐	♑	♑	♒	♓	♈	♉	♉	♊	♊	♋	♋	♌
♑	♑	♒	♓	♓	♈	♉	♊	♊	♋	♋	♋	♌	♌
♒	♓	♈	♉	♊	♊	♋	♋	♌	♌	♌	♍	♍	♎

Symbol Index

♈ Aries
♉ Taurus
♊ Gemini
♋ Cancer
♌ Leo
♍ Virgo
♎ Libra
♏ Scorpio
♐ Sagittarius
♑ Capricorn
♒ Aquarius
♓ Pisces

If your Rising Sign is ARIES (♈), you're striking looking, with bold (though not necessarily even) features, a bony angular face and fine hair. Most females with Aries Rising are of average height, but because of their "big" personalities, they often come across as taller. Aries rules the head and this could be why you're so often described as headstrong. Others see you as dynamic, assertive and impulsive, and you tend to attract people who are just as lively as you. The Aries motto is "I am" and you can come across as rather self-centred. But it can also make you appear confident and focused – both very attractive qualities. Boys love you but are sometimes put off by your forcefulness. If they are, then they're the ones who are going to lose out . . .

If your Rising Sign is TAURUS (♉), your personality is as strong and solid as your body. Females with Taurus Rising tend to be short to medium height, but make up for any lack of stature with amazing strength. You can recognize a Taurus Rising type by her square face and thick curly – usually dark – hair. Taurus rules the throat and neck and this may be why you have such a sexy and seductive voice. What people like most about you is the fact you're so down-to-earth and trustworthy – that's the way they see you anyway. The Taurus motto is "I have" and this way of thinking can cause you to be rather possessive. Unless you can curb this part of your personality – and it needs restraining because it shows itself almost as soon as you meet somebody – it could be off-putting, especially when you're trying to pull. When it comes to love, you can be a bit shy, but once you find a bloke who makes you feel secure and sexy, you'll relax and let it all hang out.

If your Rising Sign is GEMINI (♊), you're fast in every way – light on your feet, quick-thinking and an incessant chatterer – and this gives an impression of you being younger than you are. Girls with Gemini Rising tend to be medium height and very slim. You may be a tad flat-chested but you're by no means boyish – you're all woman and proud of it! You've got a cheeky expression with sparkling eyes and long arms and legs (the parts of the body ruled by Gemini). You're always on the go and never seem to finish one project before starting another. You reckon this is due to your flea-like concentration span, but other people think it's down to the fact that you're multi-talented! The Gemini motto is "I talk" and while this can be attractive to some people, it can put others right off, especially when your mouth runs away with you. Boys find you irresistible – once you learn to talk less and listen more you're bound to find the guy of your dreams.

If your Rising Sign is CANCER (♋), you have an intelligent face with twinkling eyes and a smiling mouth. Your hair is very fine and it's often either very blonde or very dark – invariably dyed. Cancer rules the bosom and you certainly have one large enough for all your mates to use as a pillow (metaphorically speaking of course!). When you first meet others, you come across as rather tough, even though underneath you're a right old softie. The Cancer motto is "I feel" and this is something which may surprise your mates. But you are, in fact, deeply sensitive and you're not doing yourself any favours by hiding this. See this quality as an asset, not a handicap, and you'll become instantly more attractive.

If your Rising Sign is LEO (♌), you have thick, wavy hair, which you like to wear back off your face. You have a lovely smiley expression and this makes you very attractive to others. As a Leo Rising female, you

may be short, but because you have good posture, your lack of stature usually goes unnoticed. Leo rules the heart and when it comes to others your heart is very big indeed. In fact, you strive to make people – especially boys – like you and would be well miffed if you discovered that someone – *anyone* – found you disagreeable. The Leo motto is "I create" and so it should be – because you're a very imaginative person. If your life ever gets boring, you'll do whatever you can to liven it up. And if you get totally tired of being you (which seems to happen from time to time), you're perfectly capable of using your creative powers to re-invent yourself. Which is fine as long as the real you doesn't get lost in the process.

If your Rising Sign is VIRGO (♍), you're a lively, chatty person with an inquisitive nature and expression. You're probably tall and, although you may be slim, you're destined to fill out as you get older! However horizontally challenged you become though, you'll always have fab legs! You may feel a bit of a wimp sometimes, but Virgo rules the stomach; maybe that's why other people see you as having plenty of guts! If something displeases you, you're certainly not going to sit there in silence – oh no. If a complaint's being made, it's more than likely Miss Virgo Rising who's making it! The Virgo motto is "I serve", which sounds a bit sad, but just illustrates how willing you are to help others. In a romantic relationship, you do run the risk of being taken for granted, so it's important that you make yourself clear at the very start. You're fussy about boyfriends, but in your view the fewer you date, the fewer you have to dump and the more fun you have.

If your Rising Sign is LIBRA (♎), you're gorgeously female and attractive, with a shapely figure and a pretty face. You're average to tall in height and have beautiful hair. Libra rules the spine and no one who knows you would ever call you spineless. In fact, you have your own particular brand of courage and forthrightness, which occasionally translates as arrogance but is often charming. This doesn't wash with your female friends, but goes down a treat with the blokes, who seem to interpret it as a kind of sexual confidence. The Libra motto is "I consider", which *should* make you discerning but in actual fact means you'll basically consider anyone! You find it very hard to say "no" to boys and this can get you into tricky situations. And although you like an easy life, you don't mind a romantic complication every now and again.

If your Rising Sign is SCORPIO (♏), you have an unusual face, with a well-defined jawline, a wide mouth and amazing eyes. Your figure is curvy (though not necessarily slim) and your hair is thick and naturally wavy. You're an inquisitive person by nature – this

may be heightened by the fact that the sign of Scorpio rules the nose! Other people see you as a real cool customer and a few may even be a bit scared of you. They know how clever and intuitive you are and because you give the impression that you're hard, they may regard you as a force to be reckoned with. Which, of course, you are . . . The Scorpio motto is "I control" and, it has to be said, you are a bit of a control freak, especially when it comes to relationships. You're the original bossy madam and won't take any nonsense from people – blokes especially – who won't do as they're told!

If your Rising Sign is SAGITTARIUS (♐), you're tall and slim, your face is oval, and your expression is open and honest. Your hair is thick and wavy and is either red or very dark. You have bright eyes, arched eyebrows and a smattering of freckles. Sagittarius rules the hips and, in other people's eyes, there's no one hipper (or hippier in some cases!) than you! You may see yourself as a cautious person, but others think you're 100 per cent reckless! Surprisingly (not to you, perhaps, but to others), the Sagittarius motto is "I think" and, contrary to popular belief, thinking is something you spend a lot of time doing. With regard to boys, as far as you're concerned, a date's a date (and usually a total riot if you've got anything to do with it!), but getting involved in a proper relationship requires much thought. You may be seen as crazy but you're not crazy enough to hurl yourself in at the deep end of love . . .

If your Rising Sign is CAPRICORN (♑), you're small and slim with a boyish air. You have thin, straight hair – dark most probably – a long face and a serious demeanour. Capricorn rules the teeth and the skeleton – perhaps that's why other people see you as someone who, once you've got your teeth into something, is like a dog with a bone! And you make no bones about letting other people see the real you either, the only difference between your opinion and theirs being that they see you as a rather sweet person. You're pretty hard on yourself, but that sort of modesty makes others warm to you. The Capricorn motto is "I learn" and that's something you do every minute of the day, especially with regard to relationships. Romantically, you aren't the sort who leaps at the chance of going out with the first bloke who fancies you: in fact, until you *really* have a boy's trust, you'll play hard to get . . .

If your Rising Sign is AQUARIUS (♒), you're very attractive with big eyes, a slightly "Roman" nose, a sharp chin and a sexy smile. You're tall and slim with long legs, narrow hips and a small bust. Aquarius rules the veins and the blood – very apt because no one likes to circulate more than you! You have loads of friends and you can somehow be someone different to each of them. You need different people for different reasons and not all the people you meet and get to know realize this. So people are often surprised when they discover that there's more to you than initially meets the eye. The Aquarian motto is "I adapt" and, it's true, you can be a complete chameleon when you need to be – socially and more so when it comes to relationships. This can confuse some blokes – especially when you jump from one personality to another! – but others (a special few, admittedly) find this a most endearing quality . . .

If your Rising Sign is PISCES (♓), you have huge glittery eyes and a figure to die for. You're easy to spot because, although you always manage to look cool, you're such a scruff: if the hem of your skirt's hanging down or buttons are missing from your shirt, you're definitely a Pisces Rising girl! Pisces rules the feet and it's no secret that you're always opening your mouth and putting your trotter in it! Generally, you're seen as someone who couldn't really care less what others think of her. But that's not entirely true (you wouldn't be reading this if it was, would you?) and your main reason for appearing that way is because you don't want people to think it's up to them to build up your self-esteem. The Piscean motto is "I believe", making you very trusting, gullible even. Many a bloke has won your heart by spouting a load of old romantic codswallop and you, like a true Pisces Rising, have fallen for it. Better luck next time; and there *will* be a next time, don't doubt it for a second . . .

The Scorpio + Rising Sign Combinations

The combination of your Sun Sign – Scorpio – with your Rising Sign is very important when it comes to your attitude towards the opposite sex.

If, for example, your **Rising Sign** is **Aries** and your Sun Sign is Scorpio, you often rush into romantic situations and then find it hard to back out when you realize you've made a mistake.

If you have a **Taurus Rising Sign** and a Scorpio Sun Sign, you're a tough cookie, but in a relationship you keep close tabs on your bloke – behaviour that's enough to frighten most of them away.

A **Gemini Rising Sign** combined with a Scorpio Sun Sign means you're a bit of a tease and find it hard to be serious about love. Boys like your flirtatiousness, but you find it hard to take things beyond that.

A **Cancer Rising Sign** combined with a Scorpio Sun Sign means you yearn for a simple life, but for some reason all your romantic relationships are destined to be very complicated.

A **Leo Rising Sign** with a Scorpio Sun Sign gives you a voracious appetite for the opposite sex. Trouble is, you can never seem to get enough of them.

If your Sun Sign is Scorpio and your **Rising Sign is Virgo**, to be truly happy, you need a boyfriend who understands your inhibitions. Only then can you feel free to be yourself.

A **Libra Rising Sign** combined with a Scorpio Sun Sign makes you generous, sexy, loving and giving – too much so at times! Watch out you don't get taken for a ride by romantically unscrupulous types.

If you're a double Scorpio – that's a **Scorpio Rising Sign** *and* a Scorpio Sun Sign – if a bloke manages to find his way to your heart, he's worked very hard to do it and deserves everything he gets.

A **Sagittarius Rising Sign** combined with a Scorpio Sun Sign means you tend to go for blokes who pose no threat to you . . . You've dated plenty of wimps, but secretly you prefer guys you can actually respect.

A **Capricorn Rising Sign** combined with a Scorpio Sun Sign means that dealings with the opposite sex can make you a bit uptight. If you can find a bloke you can trust though, you'll chill out.

An **Aquarius Rising Sign** and a Scorpio Sun Sign means you're always trying to change blokes – even ones you've just met! Not many of them appreciate this. Try taking them as they are and see what happens . . .

A **Pisces Rising Sign** and a Scorpio Sun Sign gives you a lot of romantic energy. The problem is, you tend to waste it on every bloke who so much as winks at you. You'd be much happier if you were more selective.

The Secret Life Of Scorpio

Everyone knows the characteristics of their star sign, but we all have hidden depths. Check out yours . . .

Scorpians are ruled by the powerful planet Pluto, and this gives them an aura of real purpose and cool determination. This is how you *appear* – how you actually *are* is a different matter altogether . . . Underneath that strong and forthright exterior lies a person who is terrified to allow the real personality to emerge. Deep down, although you seem confident, you're pretty insecure. And because Scorpios are so good at keeping secrets, this side of you is unlikely to be revealed. To anyone. Ever.

You seem to fear no one, but you are absolutely petrified of being controlled. You need to be in charge of your own life and can't bear the thought of anyone else having any say in it. This makes you appear tough and impervious, but that's just a shield to protect you from anyone invading your space and taking over your life. You can come across as a couldn't care-less type, and although that makes you quite a laugh, no one actually believes that you don't really care. The secret fact of the matter is, though, that sometimes you really *don't* care, and this negative attitude can lead to self-destructive behaviour in many a Scorpian.

Strengths: You seem hypercritical of others, but you're actually very understanding of other people's failings. And although typical Scorpians are considered to be really nosy, this stems from a genuine interest in others, rather than a desire for knowledge. Also, when probing, you never go too far, always sensitive to other people's feelings and always knowing when to stop.

Weaknesses: Keeping secrets for the sake of it or just to make you look more mysterious is your main weakness. And although you're a powerful person, you tend to use it to manipulate others into helping you get what you want, often without any real concern for them. Your jealousy and possessiveness, although often expressed as anger, actually stem from insecurity – a slight paranoia that nobody does – or ever will – love you.

Fears: You're frightened of people discovering that you're not as fascinating as you'd like to be. You have a fear of sharing too, a truth which is embarrassing for anyone – especially you – to face. You also worry about not being very clever: everyone you know reckons you're a right boffin, but you don't feel that you're a natural intellectual. In fact, sometimes you see yourself as pretty dunce-like. But you'd hate anyone else to see you that way . . .

Desires: You'd never admit it in a million years, but you want to be loved as much as the next person. A close one-to-one relationship isn't something you obviously strive for, but you're a romantic person (something else you keep well-hidden) and have a deep yearning for affection. You also require regular recognition and reward simply for being you. And unconditional loyalty from your nearest and dearest. And you'd quite like a dog.

Secret talent: Losing. It's a little known fact that Scorpians are actually rather noble losers. Little known because they so very rarely lose. At anything. Ever.

As a girlfriend . . . you can play whatever part your boyfriend wants you to play – to start with anyway. You're happy to allow your bloke to believe that he's the boss for a while. But if this doesn't get you what you want (i.e. ultimate total control and your own way ALL the time), you'll soon revert back to your natural, less subservient, role. If a boyfriend is supportive to you, you'll be equally supportive back. But if he lets you down or wrongs you in any way, there'll be hell to pay.

As a best friend . . . you're enthusiastic, fab company and incredibly loyal. People generally regard you as rather formal and think that you'd prefer everyone – best mate included – to book an appointment if they want to see you, but that's not true: you may be a bit that way inclined with not-so-close mates, but you always make your best buddy feel *really* welcome – even if she turns up uninvited at four in the morning! You're good at playing the agony aunt too (many people would have you down as too cool for that), and are capable of doling out sterling advice.

Scorpio In Love

Emotional Scorpio

Traditionally, Scorpio females are seen as passionate, intense and sensual, but that doesn't mean you're particularly impulsive, especially when it comes to love. In fact, although you may fall for a bloke the first time you see him, you won't make any firm commitments until you get to know him better. In a relationship, you're sensitive and somewhat insecure. You're a bit embarrassed by these (what you consider to be) bad points, and do your utmost to keep them hidden from everyone. In the same way as you're disappointed in your own faults, you find it difficult to accept those of a boyfriend (or potential boyfriend), especially if he's the sort of guy who needs a lot of emotional support.

Advice: * Be more honest about your feelings. * If you have a boyfriend, be more tolerant of his faults, especially if he's big enough to put up with yours! * Make an effort to give the men in your life the encouragement they need – not everyone is as self-reliant as you.

Practical Scorpio

You enjoy going out and having fun. Not that you enjoy spending great amounts of dosh on socializing – no, as far as you're concerned, that would be a waste. On dates, you don't like paying for the bloke, but you don't like him paying for you either. Going halves is always best as far as you're concerned. You're not one to splash out on extravagant love gifts, but if a boyfriend starts complaining about the fact that you don't appreciate him enough, you'll try to prove him wrong by splashing out on him – recklessly and generously, left, right and centre. Because you're unpredictable, you can be hard to cope with, and any bloke thinking of taking you on full-time should think very carefully. Within a relationship, you'll probably have a set of pretty strict rules, by which you expect your bloke to abide. If he's happy to do as he's told, you'll repay him by being a protective, loving and faithful girlfriend; if he rebels, then you won't be his girlfriend for long . . .

Advice: * Keep your spending on an even keel and don't use money to try to prove your affection for someone. * Try to be a bit more flexible, especially if you're thinking of getting seriously involved with someone. It's a romantic relationship, not a political campaign! * Keep your "control freak" tendencies in check. They're just not attractive.

Scorpian Love Crises

When involved in a close relationship, you need some time to yourself. You need plenty of personal space too. If your boyfriend insists on you telling him everything about yourself, then your secretive streak could cause you to withdraw from him. Despite this need, you like to know everything about your partner and hate to think that he might be hiding something from you, and can get quite paranoid and jealous as a result. This is when your rather sharp tongue goes into action and a string of cutting comments start flowing. Although you're naturally very warm, you have the ability to switch off when someone hurts or offends you. Because you're so loyal, you're unlikely to stray and when you're wronged, you're not the most forgiving of people and are quite capable of bearing a grudge for years, if not for ever! Yikes!

Advice: * Try to understand that your boyfriend is as entitled to keep secrets as you are. * Don't be too demanding – you could make a guy feel trapped. * Bite your tongue occasionally: you know you don't always mean what you say during a row, and words you use for dramatic effect can be more hurtful than you realize.

In short . . .

They Love You . . . because you're intelligent, strong, sexy and unforgettable. You're highly emotional, and take life and love seriously. You have a magnetic personality and have no trouble attracting friends and boyfriends. Your air of mystery is rather appealing too, and many people will be keen to find out what lurks beneath that hard-as-steel surface.

They Leave You . . . because you can be demanding, bitchy and obsessive. Your determination means you know what you want and if that means sometimes nabbing other girls' boyfriends, then so be it – not a good way of making yourself popular. You're stubborn too – once you've made up your mind, no one can make you change it. And then there's the jealousy. But you know all about that . . .

When You Fall In Love . . . you're the perfect girlfriend when you get what you want (i.e. total control). If you don't, you can get quite nasty. And anyone who wrongs you may be very sorry indeed.

Check this Scorpian compatibility chart to discover who you're likely to have a crush on, who you tend to date, who you fall in love with, and who's best kept as a friend. Check the key for ratings.

His Sign	You'd have a CRUSH on . . .	You tend to DATE . . .	You could LOVE . . .	You're just good FRIENDS with . . .
Aries	▼			
Taurus		❀	❤	
Gemini	❤			
Cancer			❀	
Leo		▼		❤
Virgo		❤		
Libra				▼
Scorpio				❀
Sagittarius				▼
Capricorn			❀	
Aquarius	❀			
Pisces	❤	▼	▼	

Key: ❤ = In a major way ❀ = When you're in the mood ▼ = In a minor way

Which Scorpio Are You?

As you already know, being born between October 23 and November 22 makes you a Scorpio. But contrary to popular belief, there isn't just one type of Scorpio. There are actually four. The one you are depends on your date of birth. Check below and see whether you're Miss Drama Queen, Miss Sharp, Miss Deep or Miss Charm . . .

Born October 23–29?

You're MISS DRAMA QUEEN

Often known as Libra-Scorpio Cusp and born close to the sign of Libra, you possess qualities of both signs. You're like a Libran in that you're sociable and frank, but you're like a Scorpian in that you're controlling and intense. This makes for a weird and dramatic combination: there's no way you're not going to get noticed, that's for sure! You're a real charmer and can get your own way every time. You really throw yourself wholeheartedly into everything you do and are absolutely inconsolable when things don't work out. You're serious when you want to be and see all projects through to the (sometimes) bitter end, whether they look like they're working or not.

Although you're generally pretty sensible, you have a wild side, but to many that just makes you all the more attractive . . .

Born October 29–November 6?
You're MISS SHARP

You're the most intense of all the Scorpio types, yet you're the smiliest of them all too. You have great intuition, especially when it comes to sussing out other people – something you can do successfully at a glance – and can detect, almost as soon as you meet someone, whether they're destined to be friend or enemy. You can be touchy at times and are capable of being quite nasty when you want to be, but you generally reserve this for folk who've wronged you badly. You have a fab sense of humour, but often laugh at other people's expense. You're a bit of a wind-up merchant too and often enjoy teasing others. Despite the fact you're a Scorpio, you're not overly judgmental and can be quite forgiving. Having said that, there are some things you can't forgive: you're a pretty moral person and have no time for people who behave in a deceitful or underhand way.

Born November 7–14?
You're MISS DEEP

You're the darkest of all the Scorpian types, and we're not talking hair colour here . . . You're the one with the most penetrating gaze and the real aura of mystery; and there's something about you that just screams "baaaad!" That's the image you project anyway – deep down, although you're incredibly intense and have a serious interest in all things weird and spooky, you're a pretty cool person. You're a slow mover and always wait for precisely the right moment to make your move: this applies to every area of your life – from sports through to romance. You spend a lot of type deep in thought and find yourself worrying about the most peculiar things. This sometimes prevents you from being able to join in with everyday activities – with so much to think about, it's sometimes hard just to act normal. Lighten up a bit – it'll do you the world of good.

Born November 15–22?
You're MISS CHARM

Of all the Scorpio types, you're the most attractive and charming. You make a fantastic leader, as you're able to charm others into doing exactly what you want, when you want, the way you want! You're very understanding and, although you demand commitment and loyalty from anyone who has any dealings with you, you're able to give a lot in return. The people you respect most are those who stand up to you. And although you hate criticism, it's essential you have people around you who can give their honest opinion without being scared of how you're going to react. You're a pretty sensual person and enjoy treating yourself to life's little luxuries whenever the mood takes you. Whereas Scorpios tend to be quite controlling, you are more *controlled.* This can make you very careful and scared of taking risks, which ultimately means you could lose out in certain situations. So be a bit daring sometimes.

Part 2:

Looks

It's often easy to identify a person's star sign by their looks and physique. In this chapter you'll find a description of the typical appearance of a Scorpio. If this doesn't quite fit, however, it doesn't necessarily mean you're not a typical Scorpio – it simply means that other factors, including your Rising Sign (see pages 6–19), have influenced your image. Sometimes, the combination of your Rising Sign and your Sun Sign gives you a more "mixed" look. So don't be alarmed if it doesn't sound like you. You're just that bit more intriguing!

Scorpio – The Sexy Slink!

The typical Scorpian is wiry and usually slim, with squarish shoulders and long legs. Scorpio females, although very feminine-looking, often have quite boyish figures, with flattish chests and narrow hips. You may have a slightly angular look, with sharp hip bones and prominent ankle bones. The overall impression your body gives out is an enviable one – sexiness, slinkiness and strength. So you can't complain really, can you?

Top tip: You're all too aware of what you think are bad points but could do yourself a favour by not constantly pointing them out to other people. Draw attention to your good points instead: show off your excellent physique in hip-gripping hipster trews, for example.

If you want to find out more about your body – and compare your looks to those of the other eleven signs – check the chart opposite . . . (But remember that some of you won't have the typical looks for your sign.)

Body Beautiful? Check the chart below and find out . . .

Your Sign	Height-wise you're . . .	Build-wise you're . . .	Best feature is your . . .	Worst feature is your . . .	You come across as . . .	You'd be fit if you weren't . . .
SCORPIO	MEDIUM	STOCKY	bum	legs	strong	self-destructive
SAGITTARIUS	medium/tall	athletic	thighs	hips	very fit	impatient
CAPRICORN	short	small	ankles	knees	earthy	fatalistic
AQUARIUS	tall	strong	hands	calves	unusual	unwilling
PISCES	short	thickset	chest	feet	warm	self-pitying
ARIES	medium/tall	big-boned	shoulders	scar/s(?!)	big and bold	accident prone
TAURUS	medium/tall	sturdy	neck	shoulders	cuddly	lazy
GEMINI	short/medium	slight	arms	skin	small and cute	faddy
CANCER	short/medium	chunky	skin	chest	soft	such a hypochondriac
LEO	short	slim but solid	posture	ankles	tough	arrogant
VIRGO	medium/tall	slender	legs	nails	clean	fussy
LIBRA	medium	curvy	waist	bum	sexy	indecisive

Fit For Anything!

The Scorpian body area is the reproductive system and many Scorpio girls are plagued by ailments associated with this part of their body. Problems associated with the bottom (such as piles or constipation – yikes!) are also common in Scorpians and, although these can be embarrassing, it's important to get these minor problems treated early. Bad dreams and insomnia are traditional Scorpian problems too, and these often come about because of a tendency to bottle up your feelings.

Exercise-wise, Scorpians need more than most. You might like to try martial arts, team games or kick-boxing. These sports allow you to express your aggressive streak in an acceptable way. As you're a Water Sign, you also enjoy swimming and diving.

Top tip: Although you appear cool, you're easily stressed and this can lead to physical illnesses. It's important that you sort out mental or emotional worries. Ignoring problems won't make them go away.

If you want to find out more about your health – and also see how fit the other eleven signs are – check the chart opposite . . .

Find out how to stay on top form by referring to this chart . . .

Your Sign	The most vulnerable part of your body	Most frequent illness	You have accidents . . .	Stay healthy by . . .
SCORPIO	reproductive organs	menstrual problems	with hot things	not ignoring problems
SAGITTARIUS	hips and thighs	feeling run-down	when playing sport	calming down a bit
CAPRICORN	knees	colds	because you work too hard	working less
AQUARIUS	calves and ankles	allergies	with your ankles	slowing down
PISCES	feet	being generally unwell	because your head's in the clouds	staying alert
ARIES	head	headaches	with sharp things	working out
TAURUS	throat	sore throats	because of your clumsiness	eating healthily
GEMINI	arms and hands	coughs	because you get so stressed out	doing yoga
CANCER	chest	indigestion	because you get so tired	improving your diet
LEO	back	backache	because you are always showing off	expressing yourself
VIRGO	stomach	tummy ache	because you're always so tense	relaxing more
LIBRA	kidneys	urinary infections	because you overdo it	exercising more

Fashion Victim? Not Likely!

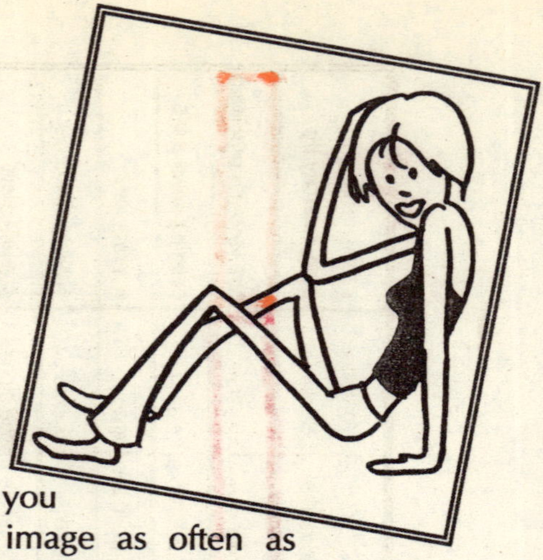

Ruled by Pluto, the planet of transformation, you like to change your image as often as possible. Your overall appearance is pretty smart and elegant, and you have the clever knack of making anything you wear look really original. Texture is very important to you – any fabrics that feel nice to the touch are the sort you go for. Silk, velvet and leather (stretch versions preferably) are your faves. You like hats, preferably ones that shield your eyes and give you a kind of mysterious look. And one sure way to spot a Scorpio by their accessories is this: they're the ones wearing sunglasses – even when the sun's not shining! Whatever you wear, though, and however you wear it, you almost always look stunning.

Top Tip: Don't allow your slightly distorted self-image to rule what you wear. Just show off that fab body!

For more details about what you wear and how you wear it – and to check out how stylish the other eleven signs are – see the chart opposite . . .

More about clothes on the chart below . . .

Your Sign	Your clothes must be . . .	The colour that suits you best is . . .	Your best thing to wear is a . . .	Your fave fabric is . . .	Favourite shop
SCORPIO	sexy	black	pair of skintight trousers	leather	French Connection
SAGITTARIUS	sporty	turquoise	wet suit!	rubber	Any sports shop
CAPRICORN	smart	brown	cool skirt suit	linen	Wallis
AQUARIUS	original	bright blue	slinky bikini	lycra	Miss Selfridge
PISCES	pretty	grey	pair of platforms	velvet	Shelly's
ARIES	a statement	red	fab hat	wool	Accessorizo
TAURUS	comfortable	blue	scruffy pair of jeans	denim	Millets
GEMINI	fashionable	yellow	sexy slip-dress	silk	Knickerbox
CANCER	feminine	sea green	long and girlie dress	lace	Benetton
LEO	noticeable	orange	tiara	lurex	Morgan
VIRGO	clean	white	pair of pinstripe trousers	cotton	Marks & Spencer
LIBRA	flirty	lilac	little A-line skirt	satin	Miss Selfridge

Sultry Scorpio!

The most noticeable Scorpian attributes are your amazing eyes – which tend to be bright and penetrating – and eyebrows, which, if left to their own devices, could get pretty unruly! You emphasize your features with quite a bit of slap: in fact, Scorpio teenagers are the most experimental of all the signs when it comes to make-up and, as a result, can often go a tad over the top. Your hair is usually dark and strong, and is pretty easy to cut. Hairdressers love the way your hair can be cut into almost any style and look magazine-photo perfect. You love changing your hair and have probably had every cut going. You're quite adventurous with hairstyles too, and regularly offer yourself up as a guinea pig to student hairdressers. Hair dyeing is popular amongst Scorpians too – and many of you choose the most outrageous shades available. If you see a girl walking down the street with green hair, chances are she's a Scorpio!

Top tip: Beware of getting too "experimental" with the slap during the day – you could frighten somebody!

If you want to find out more about the top end of your body take a peek at the chart opposite and, while you're there, check out the other eleven signs too!

Check out your face and hair on this special chart . . .

Your Sign	Your hair is great because it's . . .	On a bad-hair day it's . . .	Your face shape is . . .	Your eyes are . . .	Your mouth is . . .	Your skin is . . .
SCORPIO	abundant	floppy	broad	penetrating	sexy	normal
SAGITTARIUS	shiny	flyaway	oblong	wide apart	huge!	freckly
CAPRICORN	heavy	greasy	narrow	sleepy-looking	downturned	oily
AQUARIUS	sleek	fine	wide	sparkly	big	sensitive
PISCES	silky	sparse-looking	babyish	massive!	doll-like	translucent
ARIES	strong	frizzy	square	dark	small	ruddy
TAURUS	soft	a total riot!	rounded	baby-big	pouty	clear
GEMINI	extreme	out of control!	oval	twinkly	always moving!	a pain!
CANCER	gorgeously girlie	messy to the max!	round	small	smiley	soft
LEO	your crowning glory!	a bit OTT	square-jawed	almond-shaped	thin-lipped	dry
VIRGO	squeaky clean!	lank	long	heavy-lidded	narrow	combination
LIBRA	thick	unmanageable	heart-shaped	big and pale	perfect!	smooth

Give Yourself A Make-Over!

When it comes to making the most of your facial characteristics, make-up can play a part. In astrology, beauty has a strong connection to the elements – Fire, Earth, Air and Water. Scorpio is a Water sign, which means you prefer a sexy, feminine look. Check the characteristics of a Water sign below (you share these with the two other Water signs – Cancer and Pisces), then give yourself an elementary make-over . . .

As a WATER sign, you:

- Are incredibly romantic
- Are sensitive to the needs, moods and feelings of others
- Need a lot of love, attention and affection
- Can be moody
- Have a fantastic imagination
- Don't mind someone else taking the lead in most situations
- Like art and literature
- Can be talked into doing things you'd rather not do at all

– Are a bit secretive

Go for eye make-up in various shades of sea – it'll really bring out the colour of your irises. Emphasize your lips with pale lip colours and give your face some extra shape with clever application of blushers, shaders and highlighters. Don't bother with foundation – you really don't need it. A light dusting of translucent powder will do just fine – even for a night out on the town. Pay special attention to your hair, especially if you wear it in a long, feminine style. Short cuts look best on you, more so if your hair is fine.

Top tip: Don't use too much mascara – one coat'll do: your lashes are long and noticeable enough as they are.

Part 3:

Boy Stuff

Quiz: Who's Your Star Guy?

A lot has been said on the subject of cosmic compatibility, but you may have found that, although you're supposed to be attracted to a particular sign, you just keep going for the "wrong" ones.

This isn't because you're a glutton for punishment – in fact, you may even discover that you get on quite well with these so-called incompatible signs – but is the result of how all the planets were positioned in the heavens at the time of your birth. Although you're a Scorpio, there might have been more planets present in another sign – say, Gemini, for example – on the day you were born, causing you to take on more of the characteristics of that sign, and making you more attracted to Air and Fire signs than a typical Scorpio would be. It takes an experienced astrologer to work out an individual's birth chart (and nearly everyone's chart is different), but doing this quiz is a simple way of working out which sign is most compatible with **you**, as opposed to your sign. Try it and see . . .

1. Four different boys have the serious hots for you. They're all quite different in appearance. On looks alone, which one would you choose to go out with?

a) Serious expression, medium height with a compact physique
b) Bright-eyed, slim with a cute grin
c) Muscly bod with long limbs, amazing eyes and sexy lips
d) Athletic and masculine-looking with striking facial features and fab hair

2. At a party, you've made it clear that you fancy the guy who's standing alone on the other side of the room. Which course of action would you like him to take?
a) Ask you to dance
b) Smile encouragingly but wait for you to make the first move
c) Show his intentions through body language and meaningful stares
d) Act as cool as he can, to make it a bit more challenging for you

3. You finally get chatting. After a while, it becomes clear that he's more than keen. What happens next?
a) You ask him back to your place
b) He suggests going on somewhere else
c) He snogs you suddenly and passionately
d) Nothing – you're both too shy

4. What sort of clothes would you prefer a bloke to wear on your first date?
a) Anything that suits him
b) Anything fashionable
c) Something sporty or casual but cool-looking

d) A shirt, jacket and trousers in natural fabrics or a smart suit

5. He's taking you out for a meal. Where?

a) Pizza Express
b) McDonald's
c) At a riverside café
d) An "as much as you can eat" carvery

6. As a date, he's . . .

a) Intense, serious and a little bit shy
b) Great – he really knows how to do and say all the right things, but seems to expect a lot in return
c) Talkative, unpredictable, a great laugh
d) A great listener, romantic, giving and considerate

7. Where would you like to go on your second date?

a) Round to his place to eat a takeaway and watch TV
b) To a party or wild nightclub
c) To the cinema or theatre
d) For a picnic in the country

8. What's your attitude towards marriage?

a) It's silly, outmoded and impractical – you can't ever imagine wanting to be married
b) It stops you being yourself – and until you're convinced otherwise you're happy to stay single
c) It's lovely – romantic and secure – you can't wait to walk up that aisle
d) It's a good idea for two people who really love each other to make a commitment – when you meet the right person, you'll definitely tie the knot

9. What, to you, would be the perfect holiday?

a) A real action holiday – pony-trekking, mountaineering or something like that
b) As long as there's a reasonable amount of luxury and you can spend time relaxing, you don't care where you go
c) Anywhere you can sample a bit of culture, unusual food and drink and feel all the more enlightened for it
d) Somewhere that stimulates your imagination and leaves you feeling mentally refreshed

10. Which colour is your favourite?

a) Bright yellow, violet or electric blue
b) Bright red, orange, gold or turquoise
c) Pale blue, pink, any shade of green, navy, brown or white
d) Grey, pale blue, silver, dark red, black or sea green

Now work out your scores, making a note of how many F's, E's, A's and W's you get . . .

1. a – E; b – A; c – W; d – F
2. a – F; b – E; c – W; d – A
3. a – W; b – A; c – F; d – E
4. a – W; b – A; c – F; d – E
5. a – A; b – F; c – W; d – E
6. a – E; b – F; c – A; d – W
7. a – E; b – F; c – A; d – W
8. a – A; b – F; c – W; d – E
9. a – F; b – E; c – A; d – W
10. a – A; b – F; c – E; d – W

If you scored mostly F, go to the FIRE section.
If you scored mostly E, go to the EARTH section.
If you scored mostly A, go to the AIR section.
If you scored mostly W, go to the WATER section.

(In the event of a "tie" – i.e., you score equally on two or more sections – you can go to both or all sections indicated and be ultimately equally attracted to two or more different star signs.)

Fire

Fire sign guys are:

* Energetic
* Warm
* Fun-loving
* Passionate
* Enthusiastic
* A little bit crazy

Sound like your type? Now answer this simple question:

Which of the following statements do you most agree with?

a) When I go on a date, I like a guy to be spontaneous and passionate. If he wants more than a goodnight peck on the cheek that's just fine by me.
b) When I go out with a guy, I like to be treated with a substantial amount of respect. I like to have fun, but I hate being rushed and like to take relationships one step at a time.
c) All I want from a boyfriend is a good time. If he's

happy, I'm happy. I've no intentions of getting heavy with a guy – that's the best way to send him running.

*If you answered a) the guy for you is an **Aries**. To find out more about him, turn to page 51.*

*If you answered b) the guy for you is a **Leo**. To find out more about him, turn to page 62.*

*If you answered c) the guy for you is a **Sagittarius**. To find out more about him, turn to page 72.*

Earth

Earth sign guys are:

* Hard-working
* Faithful
* Practical
* Loyal
* Down-to-earth
* A little bit sensible

Sound like your type? Now answer this simple question:

Which of the following qualities do you believe to be the most important in a boyfriend?

a) Serious sexiness

b) A fab sense of humour

c) Immense cleverness

*If you answered a) the guy for you is a **Taurus**. To find out more about him, turn to page 54.*

*If you answered b) the guy for you is a **Virgo**. To find out more about him, turn to page 64.*

*If you answered c) the guy for you is a **Capricorn**. To find out more about him, turn to page 75.*

Air

Air sign guys are:

* Talkative
* Sociable
* Changeable
* Unpredictable
* Interesting
* A little bit "bonkers"

Sound like your type? Now answer this simple question:

Which of the following dates would you prefer?

a) Going to a posh restaurant for dinner, then to see your fave band, then to the best nightclub in town to rave until the early hours.

b) Spending a day in the country, having a snog in a cornfield, followed by supper at an Olde Worlde Inne and a romantic train ride home, watching the sunset through the dusk.

c) Having a champagne breakfast (OK, so you may be under eighteen, but this is fantasy-land here) in a hot air balloon, a nice walk by the river, then on to see a fascinating film at your local cinema.

If you answered a) the guy for you is a ***Gemini****. To find out more about him, turn to page 56.*

If you answered b) the guy for you is a ***Libra****. To find out more about him, turn to page 67.*

If you answered c) the guy for you is an ***Aquarius****. To find out more about him, turn to page 78.*

Water

Water sign guys are:

* Sensitive
* Sentimental
* Mysterious
* Secretive
* Intense
* A little bit weird

Sound like your type? Now answer this simple question:

Which of the following holidays would you like best?

a) A relaxing holiday by the sea, somewhere peaceful, picturesque and romantic.
b) A luxurious holiday in a historical setting, where there are lots of old ruins and places to explore.
c) A sailing holiday in a faraway, beautiful, uncrowded and exotic place.

If you answered a) the guy for you is a ***Cancer****. To find out more about him,* *turn to page 59.*

If you answered b) the guy for you is a ***Scorpio****. To find out more about him,* *turn to page 70.*

If you answered c) the guy for you is a ***Pisces****. To find out more about him,* *turn to page 80.*

Astro-Boys

So you've found your ideal romantic partner . . . Well, now's the time to check him out good and proper.

Aries (March 20–April 19)

He's a hero . . . because he's really popular and has a zillion mates you can flirt with. Also . . .

* He's honest and straightforward
* He's very affectionate
* He's sexy to the max
* He loves to spring little surprises on you
* Everyone thinks he's fab
* He's a top snogger!!

He's a zero . . . when he acts creepy around girls (he could smarm for Britain!) and two-times (sometimes three-times) girlfriends. Plus . . .

* He's just too bossy
* He's always ogling other girls
* He tells the occasional "white" lie
* He's a bit of a stirrer
* He won't wait for anyone or anything
* He'll never love you more than he loves himself

Personality Alert!

No matter how much he likes you, you'll never be his number one priority. Because his number one priority is (as if you haven't guessed) . . . himself!

He looks great . . . because he's got a fab body – not an ounce of fat! – a chiselled, model-like face and a sexy expression. He's slim and muscular with wide shoulders and snakey hips. Arien males usually have thick, dark, well-styled hair which they're always touching. Facially, they look much like the animal that represents their sign – a ram! – especially in profile, with a long straight nose, chiselled cheekbones, beetly eyebrows and small mouth and chin. He likes fashionable clothes in bright colours and although he generally favours the sporty look, he will dress up smart if the occasion requires it.

He's a state . . . because he's a bit of a poseur and tends to overdo it with the "designer" labels. (Also, if you don't like the facial characteristics of a ram, then he may not be your cup of tea . . .)

Meet him . . .
- wherever there's a football.
- getting on down at the grooviest club in town.
- in McDonald's – on either side of the counter.

Impress him by . . . being totally upfront. If you fancy him, don't be shy: tell him. He'll love you for it! To catch his attention, wear something bright (in his team's colours preferably). If he compliments you, be grateful, but don't let him see you flirt with other guys – that's something he can't stand.

If you can't be bothered to do the running . . . then that won't be a problem. He loves the thrill of the chase, so once he gets wind of you fancying him, he'll be straight in there! He certainly doesn't beat around the metaphorical bush when it comes to chatting up girls, so chances are he'll just come and tell you if he fancies you (unfortunately, he'll also tell you just as loud and clear if he doesn't!) He's a great snogger – and he knows it – so he may just lunge for your lips before he's even spoken to you! Scary or what?!

Keep him by . . . never bossing him around (especially in front of his mates); being mega-appreciative when he's nice to you; telling him you love him at every opportunity; not flirting with other blokes; showing him what a totally cool and busy chick you are!

Dump him when . . . you find him snogging your best mate. (And you will.)

Love match: If you're a Leo, a Libran or a Sagittarian, you're putty in his hands!

Top Arien totty: Mark Hamilton (Ash), Damon Albarn, Linford Christie, Coree (Damage), Will Mellor, Robert Downey Jnr and Paul Nicholls.

Taurus (April 20–May 20)

He's a hero . . . because of his loving, gentle nature. He's loyal to those he loves and, whether you're his mate or his girlfriend, he'll stand by you at all times. Also . . .

* He has masses of sex appeal (and doesn't even know it!)
* He'll listen to your problems all day and all night
* He's modest, kind and reliable
* He makes you go all quivery whenever he touches you
* He's very romantic

He's a zero . . . because he's the King Of Self-Indulgence and barely notices you exist sometimes! Plus . . .

* He's a bit of a couch potato
* His temper can get out of control
* He can't always keep up with you
* His moods are too much to take sometimes
* He can be self-obsessed
* He's hideously stubborn

Personality Alert!

His worst nightmare comes true when you finally discover that, underneath it all, he is in fact very boring! Oh no!!

He looks great . . . because he's super-cuddly and mega-cute. And he's got a million woolly jumpers that he won't mind lending you (only when you're his girlfriend of course . . .). He has a clear complexion, a sweet little mouth and gorgeous eyes. Most Taurus guys love clothes – and while they like the idea of looking trendy, they tend to dress down, preferring comfortable clothes in natural colours and fabrics. Show him a little something in Lycra and he'll run a mile!

He's a state . . . mainly because sometimes he just can't be bothered and, looks-wise, could give Swampy a run for his money! Also, he's a right old sloucher – it's sometimes hard to tell the difference between a Taurean bloke on a sofa and a sack of spuds!

Meet him . . .

- round at his place (he doesn't get out much!)
- round his mate's house (he rarely has more than one close male friend).
- in the local greasy caff (he really enjoys a good fry-up!)

Impress him by . . . enjoying lazing around as much as he does and taking the lead when it comes to getting physical. He's very tactile, so when you're there on the sofa with him, touch him at every opportunity. He likes girls who are relaxed and know how to have a good time. He's a bit worried about being boring and stupid though, so don't tease him in any way – especially in front of his mates. (Or should we say mate?!)

If you can't be bothered to do the running . . . you could have a problem. He's a shy guy at the best of times, so don't expect him to bowl you over with his bird-pulling tactics. If he so much as smiles at you across a crowded room, he thinks he's being pushy. He takes his time working out who he fancies, but once he's made up his mind, he'll make sure he's near you at all times, giving you the chance to make *your* move on *him*. Very subtle . . .

Keep him by . . . having a fab sense of humour; being open about your feelings; not taking the mickey out of him; not snogging or fighting him in public; giving him the time and space he needs, especially when it comes to making decisions.

Dump him when . . . he asks for his jumpers back.

Love match: If you're a Virgo, Scorpio or Capricorn, you're the girl for him.

Top Taurean totty: Jas Mann (Babylon Zoo), Jay Darlington (Kula Shaker), Harry Enfield, Lance (N-Sync), Emilio Estevez and Sean Conlon (5ive) .

Gemini (May 21–June 20)

He's a hero . . . because he's a social chameleon and you can take him anywhere! He has opinions on every subject and loves a chat. He's also broad-minded, but PC at the same time. Also . . .

* He gets on with all your mates
* He's a real good laugh
* He's ever so romantic
* Life's never dull when he's around
* He's a big kid

He's a zero . . . because, as he's so easily bored, he can make you feel boring! He's moody to the max and can be horribly irritable. He also "forgets" dates and can be immature. Plus . . .

* He's too demanding
* He's totally unpredictable
* He won't stop flirting
* He thinks nothing of dating two (or even three) girls at a time
* He's a huge show-off

Personality Alert!

He may look like butter wouldn't melt in his mouth, but he's the best liar in the zodiac. So be prepared to be foiled!

He looks great . . . because his tall, slim physique makes him look quite model-like. He has a sweet face, with twinkly eyes and a very naughty expression.

He's a state . . . because his sense of "style" (if you can call it that) leaves a lot to be desired. He loves to be trendy, but gets it totally wrong sometimes and ends up looking like a rather sad fashion victim. And what's with all the daft hats?! If any bloke makes you feel like calling the Fashion Police, it'll be Mr Gemini!

Meet him . . .

- at the trendiest hot spot in town.
- on a bus, train or plane.
- in a mobile phone showroom.

Impress him by . . . telling him you fancy him in five different languages (he likes clever – and straight-talking – chicks!) or asking him to help you with *The Times* crossword. And when you get chatting to him, make sure you laugh at all his jokes (even the totally surreal ones!) Once you've located him, you must play it as cool as he does. Never show your jealous side (if you've got one) and try to maintain an air of mystery.

If you can't be bothered to do the running . . . don't expect him to come running after you. This guy never makes much effort when it comes to pulling – mainly because he doesn't have to. His looks mean that you can't fail to notice him, but if he fancies you, he will use his ability to bewitch you from a distance, without saying a word. A Gemini boy can make you feel "drawn" to him and, no matter how shy you are, you'll suddenly find that you're the one doing all the work! Note: once in his clutches it may be hard to escape!

Keep him by . . . being very understanding (telepathic preferably!); staying faithful (even when he's not!);

putting up with his moods; spending most of your time together talking about him.

Dump him when . . . he stops returning your phone calls, and starts making up crap excuses about where he's been and what he's been doing.

Love match: He can only have a long-term relationship with Libran, Sagittarian or Aquarian girls.

Top Geminian totty: Lenny Kravitz, Johnny Depp, Noel Gallagher and Jason Brown (5ive).

Cancer (June 21–July 22)

He's a hero . . . because, most of the time, he's kind, caring, sensitive and trustworthy. He also cooks a mean roast dinner! Also . . .

* He's mega-romantic
* He'll never let you down
* He really understands you
* He'll love you more than anyone has ever loved you
* He's honest and sincere
* He won't hear a bad word said against you

He's a zero . . . because he's mega-crabby, secretly compares his girlfriends to his mum (and it's unlikely any of them will live up to *her* angelic image), and can be unbelievably selfish. Plus . . .

* He spoils all your fun
* He winds you up like nobody else
* He's a bit of a drama queen!
* He thinks he's always in the right
* He wants everyone to feel sorry for him all the time

Personality Alert!

He can be clingier than cling film and twice as suffocating! Shaking him off could prove difficult.

He looks great . . . with his high cheekbones and charming smile. His clothes are generally pretty cool, and so they should be: they cost enough! He has a rather distinctive face with well-defined features and a friendly expression.

He's a state . . . when he takes the "baggy" look too far and the crotch of his jeans is hovering way below knee level! And, although he's probably slim, he's able to pile on the pounds easily – and, sometimes when he gets involved in a relationship, he lets himself go and gets to be a right old bloater!

Meet him . . .

– beside the seaside (or anywhere there's water really).
– in an amusement arcade (he loves computer games).
– at home, eating a slap-up tea.

Impress him by . . . telling him loads of intimate stuff about yourself and avoiding asking him any nosy questions about himself. Also, as Cancer boys love a snack, share your Rolos with him and he'll be yours for life!

If you can't be bothered to do the running . . . it could take some time before he'll chase you. He's a bit shy so he's not going to make the first move, no matter how many hints you give him. If he even vaguely suspects that you don't like him he'll run a mile. If you make the first move, he'll respond quickly and usually positively. Most Cancer guys, once they're sure of your feelings, can get very romantic and will try to woo you in all the traditional ways – with flowers, poetry, love letters . . . the works!

Keep him by . . . telling him you'll love him forever; being a total tower of strength; standing up for him even when you think he's in the wrong; always taking his opinions and his ideas seriously; being faithful; making him believe he can trust you.

Dump him when . . . he stops and gazes wistfully in the window of Ratners every time you go shopping!

Love match: When he settles, it'll be with a Scorpian, Capricornian or Piscean chick.

Top Cancerian totty: Jamie Redknapp, George Michael, Keith Duffy and Shane Lynch (Boyzone), Tom Cruise, Terry Caldwell (East 17), Prince William and Ross Kemp (EastEnders).

Leo (July 23–August 22)

He's a hero . . . because he's manly, sexy and in control. He's also very generous and great fun to go out with. Also . . .

* He loves a good cuddle
* He buys you tons of pressies
* He's majorly optimistic
* He'll take good care of you
* He'll always forgive you

He's a zero . . . because he's a pain-in-the-butt show-off with an ego the size of Edinburgh! Plus . . .

* He's always telling you what to do
* He needs constant flattery
* He fancies himself more than he fancies you
* He's too demanding
* He expects you to drop all your mates in favour of him

Personality Alert!

He can be totally embarrassing – especially when he insists on giving you massive snogs in public!

He looks great . . . as he's a fine figure of a lad with broad shoulders and lush hair. He may not be that lofty, but his posture is good and he strides around in a very "tall" and purposeful way. His face is unusual and usually has something feline about it – slightly slanty eyes perhaps . . . or whiskers maybe! (A lot of post-adolescent Leo guys favour a goatee beard!)

He's a state . . . because he wears too much jewellery (how many chains can a guy drape round one neck?), his hair is too coiffeured (à la The Bee Gees circa 1976), and his "look" is just a bit too considered (i.e. you can tell he spends hours in front of the mirror).

Meet him . . .

- at a gig (one where his band is playing).
- at the theatre (he'll be the star of the show).
- at the cash-point machine (he always has a good wad on him!).

Impress him by . . . flattering him all the time (it'll get you everywhere!) and by being totally committed, dependent even (he likes a girl who brings out the chauvinist in him!). Flattery gets you absolutely everywhere with this guy – no line is too corny! Compliment him on his clothes, his hair, his bike – anything! – and he'll be instantly smitten. He likes lively, upfront girls, so skulking around waiting for him to make the first move won't impress him. Oh – and if you want to make him yours, you should be supermodel gorgeous (although preferably slightly lower on the beauty scale than himself – he hates to be outshone!).

If you can't be bothered to do the running . . . he's sure as hell too proud to make a move on you. He's so wrapped up in himself, he won't have time to waste chasing girls. If he fancies you, he'll let you know in quite an obvious way but will then sit back and expect you to do all the running. His ego won't allow him to do it any other way!

Keep him by . . . being naturally beautiful (he doesn't ask for much, this guy); always paying your way (he's generous but hates being taken for granted); never criticizing him; being ready to party at the drop of a hat.

Dump him when . . . he starts telling you that, more than anything, you've always been a really good friend to him.

Love match: He'll find long-term love with a Sagittarian, Aquarian or Arien female.

Top Leo totty: Matt Le Blanc, Sean Moore (Manic Street Preachers), Arnie Schwarzenegger, Fatboy Slim, David Duchovny and Christian Slater.

Virgo (August 23–September 22)

He's a hero . . . with a brilliant sense of humour – he's the wittiest sign of the zodiac – and a helpful, sympathetic and protective nature. Highly desirable. Also . . .

* He's very clever
* He's extremely cool
* He's never late
* He likes a laugh
* He's fussy about who he goes out with – if he's chosen you, you *must* be special!

He's a zero . . . because his analytical and critical nature can be off-putting. He can also be a bit grumpy and over-demanding. Plus . . .

* He's always putting you down
* He makes a right song and dance about everything you do
* He's a bit mean
* He thinks you're lucky to be in any way connected to him
* He rarely says anything nice to you
* He's emotionally repressed

Personality Alert!

He can pick so many holes in you that you could feel like a colander by the end of your first date!

He looks great . . . with his bright eyes, faintly "amused" expression and spotlessly clean and immaculately ironed clothes. Virgo blokes are attractive – in their own quirky little way. Some look a bit delicate – all knees, elbows and knobbly bits! Most have narrow faces, bright eyes, long noses, thin lips, pointy chins and fine hair. He wears clean, well-pressed clothes in natural fabrics (such as cotton, wool and silk) – classy!

He's a state . . . only first thing in the morning. And even then, his 'jamas are only a teensy bit crumpled! His only other fashion crime is that he does seem to favour narrow-legged trousers and will insist on donning his "drainpipes" even when everyone else is flaunting their flares.

Meet him . . .

– in the supermarket (he's the one referring to a really long list).
– in the chemist's or health food shop (he's always got something wrong with him and in need of cures).
– in the hairdresser's (he has his hair trimmed at least twice a month!)

Impress him by . . . being a "quality bird" (he hates cheapness of any description) and not being coarse or over the top when attempting to pull him. Once you get chatting, don't laugh when he harps on about all his ailments (and he has lots); try to stay chirpy (if there's any moaning to be done, *he* wants to be the one doing it!); and make a point of being very (*very*) interested in everything he says.

If you can't be bothered to do the running . . . don't worry – as long as he's confident you like him, he'll have no qualms about making a move on you. If a Virgo bloke is trying to pull you, you may not notice at first – he's *that* subtle (some would say devious!) When chatting you up, he'll try all his best one-liners on you and have you in fits of laughter. Once he's got you hooked though, he gets really serious and, to some girls, this can be impressive in itself.

Keep him by . . . being 100 per cent devoted; allowing him to impress other girls with his witty quips (he's not flirting – honest!); never gossiping about him with your mates; being mega-sensitive when it comes to his feelings; not springing surprises on him.

Dump him when . . . you start to feel like one of his many ailments.

Love match: If he wants to meet his match, he should be looking for a Capricorn, Pisces or Taurus.

Top Virgoan totty: Keanu Reeves, Charlie Sheen, Hugh Grant, Paul Winterhart (Kula Shaker), Jarvis Cocker, Liam Gallagher and Jimmy Constable (911).

Libra (September 23– October 22)

He's a hero . . . because he has very strong beliefs and is a great mediator. When you come over all "damsel in distress", he's the guy to save you.

Also . . .

* He's sensitive, sensual and sexy
* He'll tell you all the things you want to hear
* He's a great listener
* He's very polite
* He's great to go out with
* His moods are pretty constant
* He's pretty smart

He's a zero . . . because he's vain, superficial, manipulative and so charming he makes you feel sick sometimes. Plus . . .

* He flirts too much
* He's lazy

* He talks a right load of rubbish at times
* He's horribly indecisive
* He's *sooo* impractical
* He's a bit of a fibber

Personality Alert!

He's a sneaky, smarmy snake-in-the-grass, who'll two-time you at the first opportunity. (Oh dear. And he seemed like such a nice chap . . .)

He looks great . . . because he's got dimples, a cheeky smile and a lovely pouty mouth. He looks after his clothes well – even his oldest trackie pants look brand new. His body is athletic-looking, his posture is good and his movements are graceful. He dresses to suit the occasion and can go from looking smart to scruffy, from frumpy to fashionable in a matter of hours. *Fact:* you can spot a Libran bloke by his shoes – he almost always wears baseball boots or trainers.

He's a state . . . because he's got such bad colour coordination, you'd need sunglasses to look at some of his "ensembles". And what's with the baseball cap – is it welded to his head or what?

Meet him . . .
– on a computer course.
– at an after-school/work discussion group.
– in the pet shop (he adores animals!)

Impress him by . . . telling him you're on intimate terms with Robbie Williams and most of All Saints (he loves a lig!), then inviting him to a celebrity bash. (It's not your fault if they all fail to turn up!) If you're interested in this bloke, then above all else you must be easy-going and intelligent. If you're daft or demanding, he won't want to know. He likes a girl to be independent so impress him by parpling on about your numerous extra-curricular activities and your bulging-at-the-seams social diary. To clinch the deal, compliment his looks and comment on his great wit and insight. He's a sucker for flattery!

If you can't be bothered to do the running . . . you won't have to wait long for him to come after you. He'll use his charm, good looks and generosity to attract your attention. He's an expert chatter-upper, so half the time you won't even know he's on the pull. He'll flatter you, be truly fascinated by everything you say and laugh his noggin off at all your jokes.

Keep him by . . . being caring and supportive; allowing him space for his own "interests" (this may or may not include dating other girls. Yikes!); having friends and hobbies of your own; being funny; paying him lots of compliments and springing lavish surprises on him.

Dump him when . . . the flowers he sends you start smelling of guilt.

Love match: He needs a girl who understands him – an Aquarian, Arien or Geminian perhaps.

Top Libran totty: Declan Donnelly, Brett Anderson (Suede), Will Smith and Zac (Zachary Walker) Hanson from Hanson.

Scorpio (October 23–November 22)

He's a hero . . . because he's dynamic, caring and totally unshockable. And, although he's a perfectionist, he's remarkably understanding when it comes to other people's shortcomings. Also . . .

* He's quick-witted and clever
* He can give you everything you need
* He'll really look after you
* He makes you believe he knows you better than you know yourself
* He's got a sexy and mysterious aura
* He can help you get whatever you want

He's a zero . . . because his overwhelming need to be in control can be scary. He's also capable of being hideously self-destructive if things don't go his way. Plus . . .

* He's capable of being dangerously possessive
* He's at the mercy of that green-eyed monster
* He wants to know everything about you but tells you very little about himself
* He thinks he's never wrong
* He makes out he's a real one-woman guy, but he can be unfaithful on a whim

Personality Alert!

He's such a control freak, he'll have you on a dog lead

and signed up for Crufts as soon as you can say "Yes, master (woof!)".

He looks great . . . thanks to those deeply gorgeous eyes and that intense stare. A Scorpio bloke can take on many outward appearances but he's usually casual-but-smartly dressed, well built (though not always tall), with broad shoulders and chest, little snakey hips and a cute butt! He's likely to have a wide forehead, a thick neck, bushy eyebrows and hairy arms(!) All very nice (if you like that kind of thing . . .)

He's a state . . . because sometimes he goes too far with the old macho image and ends up looking like a lumberjack! Plus . . . *Fact:* if a guy has bow-legs, chances are he's a Scorpio!

Meet him . . .
- on the rugby pitch (he loves a scrum or two!)
- in the bookshop, looking for a good thriller or detective novel.
- in bed, watching *Inspector Morse* videos.

Impress him by . . . finding out everything about him before you actually speak to him, then pretending you're psychic! This guy is pretty tricky to ensnare because he has extremely high expectations. He likes to do his own thing so won't necessarily be attracted to you simply because *you* like playing pool too. And anyway, he'd rather you were there in a cheerleader role than in a directly competitive one. If you can prove you're discreet, uncritical and not in the tiniest bit jealous, he *may* just give you a second glance.

If you can't be bothered to do the running . . . that's not a problem – for a short while anyway. If he hears you have the hots for him, he'll be secretly flattered but won't be that obvious in his quest to pull you. His favourite pulling technique is staring. Then he'll take off his shades and stare some more. If that doesn't have the desired effect (i.e. you slavering over him in a matter of minutes), he'll forget all about you and move on to someone who's more receptive to his magnetism.

Keep him by . . . being faithful; being realistic rather than romantic; telling him you're the luckiest girl in the world (why? Because you're going out with him of course!); and never accusing him of being in the wrong (even when he is).

Dump him when . . . he starts blaming you for his self-destructive behaviour.

Love match: The only girls he's truly happy with are Pisceans, Taureans and Cancerians.

Top Scorpian totty: Alonza Bevan (Kula Shaker), Ethan Hawke, Leonardo DiCaprio, Ike (Clarke Isaac) Hanson from Hanson and Alex James (Blur).

Sagittarius (November 23–December 21)

He's a hero . . . because he's honest and fair-minded, always sees the best in people and would never bear a grudge against anyone. He's also a genuinely

interesting person and is excellent company. Also . . .

* He can always cheer you up
* He's never boring
* He's always got a smile on his face
* He's your best friend
* Nothing's dull when he's around

He's a zero . . . because he's impatient, reckless and argumentative. And he's always telling people how to run their lives when it's *his* life – more than anyone's – that needs sorting. Plus . . .

* He always seems to be putting his foot in it
* He's really immature
* You can't rely on him
* He can't sit still for a minute
* He's got a bit of an unpredictable temper
* He's incapable of being faithful

Personality Alert!

He's about as easy to lean on as a cloud!

He looks great . . . but only by accident! When you meet him, the first thing you'll notice is his gorgeous legs and bum. If you can drag your eyes upwards, you may notice his big mouth, sparkling eyes and cute little hair "do".

He's a state . . . most of the time. In fact, even on a good day, he looks as if he's covered his body in glue and run backwards through his wardrobe! He's got absolutely no dress sense and anything he wears is usually mismatched, crumpled or just plain grubby. What a scruff!

Meet him . . .

– dreamily reading the special offer cards in travel agents' windows.
– on holiday.
– at a wild party.

Impress him by . . . doing something pretty spectacular – it's the only way you'll ever get him away from the other girls. He likes girls who are as free and easy as he is, so if you're ready to do crazy, impulsive things at a moment's notice, you may be the girl for him. He's not keen on girls who are too grown-up, so coming on all sophisticated with him just won't work.

If you can't be bothered to do the running . . . he's more than happy to do it. He desperately needs to be liked and he'll do anything – including lie – to impress you. He'll try to be cool, but he's not. But his most successful tactic is playing the bumbling idiot – it works a treat every time and may even work on you!

Keep him by . . . telling him you're perfectly happy about having an "open" relationship; constantly reminding him that you've "never felt like this about anyone before" while at the same time not putting any restraints on him (tricky, eh?); inviting him on all your girls' nights out (he won't go but he'll appreciate being asked).

Dump him when . . . he says he's going away for the weekend, then disappears for three months.

Love match: If you're an Arien, Geminian or Leo you'll find this guy totally irresistible.

Top Sagittarian totty: Michael Owen, Ryan Giggs, Gary Lineker, Brad Pitt, Neil Codling (Suede) and Jamie Theakston.

Capricorn (December 22–January 20)

He's a hero . . . because he's brave, realistic and is a great person to turn to for advice. Also, if you're feeling low, he's just the guy to give your ego a boost. Also . . .

* He's loyal
* He always lets you win arguments
* He'll never forget your birthday (or your mum's come to that!)
* You can talk to him about practically anything

He's a zero . . . because he's narrow-minded and refuses to see things from other people's points of view. And, although painfully modest on the surface, deep down he's a tad full of himself. Plus . . .

* He has an overdeveloped dark side (oo-er!)
* He tends to take things the wrong way

* He can be a bit predictable
* He's very insecure
* He won't take any risks
* He's a bit tight with his cash

Personality Alert!

He could drive you mad with his incessant talk of computers!

He looks great ... in his good-quality, expensive gear. He wears a lot of his fave colour – black. But he looks best when his girlfriend dresses him. Because he's a tad conservative, he doesn't particularly stand out, but once you're pointed in his direction, you'll realize how attractive he can be with his bright, intelligent-looking eyes and pixie-ish face.

He's a state . . . because he can't do a thing with his hair! It's stuck to his head like seaweed to a rock! It's unlikely that you'll be overwhelmed by this guy's looks, because although he's *kind* of cute, he's not what you'd call a "stunner". And why does he look so *worried* all the time?

Meet him . . .

– at the railway station (he's a closet trainspotter!).
– buying CDs (he's a tune-aholic – although he's more Bach than Backstreet!).
– in the library, studying for a "project" (he's such a swot!).

Impress him by . . . asking him how fax machines

work or asking him out by e-mail. (He loves girls with an interest in technology.) He likes quiet, sophisticated girls and won't be impressed by anyone loud, crude or raucous. So you can forget about telling him your fave dirty jokes! He likes you to be interested in his hobbies and won't take too kindly to any teasing.

If you can't be bothered to do the running . . . he's not a natural flirt so won't go out of his way to go after you. Most Capricorn guys favour the subtle approach and would rather get a mutual mate to introduce you than approach you. Once he's got your attention, he'll try to blind you with his vast intellect. If you're the type of girl who prefers brain to brawn, this just might work.

Keep him by . . . not yawning when he's talking technology; getting engaged on your first date (he likes to feel secure in a relationship); giving him privacy when he needs it; being quiet and refined; not moaning about his hobbies, even if he spends more time on them than he does on you.

Dump him when . . . you discover his little black book contains more than just the numbers of trains . . .

Love match: If you're a Taurean, a Virgoan or a Cancerian, get on in there!

Top Capricornian totty: Denzel Washington, Tim (Ash), Jim Carrey and Gary Barlow.

Aquarius (January 21–February 18)

He's a hero . . . because he's loyal and deep-thinking. He finds people fascinating and is incredibly observant. If you've got any questions about human behaviour, he's the guy to ask! Also . . .

* He's amusing
* He never seems to get tired
* Everyone likes him
* He'd never two-time you
* He's strong and independent
* He really seems to understand you

He's a zero . . . because he thinks it's cool to make jokes at other people's expense. He can be honest to the point of tactlessness and although he thinks his bizarre brand of humour is hilarious, very few people would agree. Plus . . .

* He can be cold and unfeeling sometimes
* He's a tad full of himself
* You never know where he is
* It's hard to know where he's going, where he's been or where he's coming from
* He's 100 per cent bonkers!

Personality Alert!

You may love him cracking jokes, but you'll soon go off it when you realize that he just won't stop!

He looks great . . . because, although he's not traditionally good-looking, he has an interesting and unusual face with wide-apart eyes, prominent cheekbones, a wide smiley mouth and a cute nose. When it comes to clothes, he has a rather distinctive style all of his own.

He's a state . . . *because* he's got a rather distinctive style all of his own!

Meet him . . .

– at the gym. (He likes to keep his lithe physique in peak condition – just in case he's called upon to save the world or something . . .)
– at the cinema, checking out the latest arty, subtitled film.
– collecting for charity. (So don't worry about going out looking for him – he'll be on your doorstep, rattling a collection box at you, before you know it!)

Impress him by . . . being cool and independent. The less girlie you are, the better. Mind you, he's a sucker for a bit of recognition so, when you first meet him, tell him you remember his fantastic performance in the Year 8 school play, and he'll be all yours! He has an intense dislike of soppy, overly romantic females, so forget the elaborately wrapped chocs and buy him a chip butty instead!

If you can't be bothered to do the running . . . he can run fast enough for you both. To get your attention, he'll do impressions, tickle you with his wit and "wisdom" and make a million silly faces. He'll also play practical jokes on you and rib you mercilessly. He'll ask loads of personal questions but won't tell you much in return. If you like a laugh-a-minute man of mystery, then Mr Aquarius is sure to win your heart!

Keep him by . . . not questioning his movements; tolerating his strange little "quirks"; putting up with his rowdy mates; never getting hysterical; not gossiping; smiling constantly.

Dump him when . . . he insists on making you the butt of all his awful jokes.

Love match: Gemini, Leo and Libra lasses just can't say no to him.

Top Aquarian totty: Robbie Williams.

Pisces (February 19–March 19)

He's a hero . . . because he's caring, helpful and, even as a mate, he'll always be there when you need him. As a boyfriend, he's really romantic, but that doesn't stop him from being a bit of a crazy party animal. Also . . .

* He's really loving

* He knows how to have a good time
* He's deep and philosophical
* He's always making romantic gestures
* He'll take you to fantasy-land (if you fancy it)
* He'd do anything for you

He's a zero . . . because his self-esteem is so low, it can be a drag always having to pump up his ego for him. Also, when it comes to practical stuff, he's just useless! (Q: How many Pisceans does it take to change a light bulb? A: Ten – nine to form a search party to go looking for a handyman and one to write a poem about it!) Plus . . .

* He's too scatty
* He doesn't know which way up he is
* He allows others to take advantage of him
* He's impressed by the dodgiest people
* He can't make a decision to save his life!

Personality Alert!

He's a dithering dreamer and you could get fed up constantly trying to pull his dappy little head out of the clouds.

He looks great . . . in second-hand clothes. He's got a really sweet face with large, watery-looking eyes, dimples, a long nose and a pouty mouth. His hair is baby-soft and tends to have a public schoolboy floppiness about it. He's got excellent posture (you'll never see a Piscean guy slouching), is naturally graceful (get him up on a catwalk!) and is a lovely little mover (see him go on that dance floor!). He likes comfy clothes in unusual styles and natural fabrics.

He's a state . . . when he tries to look smart: it's just not him!

Meet him . . .
– at a jumble sale or charity shop. (He may even work there.)
– at the local swimming baths or aquarium. (Pisces *is* the sign of the fish.)
– at a publishing house, trying to get them to publish his poems.

Impress him by . . . buying or making him a present and posting it to him. Once he gets the message that you fancy him, he'll ask you out. (So make sure he knows it's from you . . .) Once you get chatting to him, try not to be too argumentative – he hates confrontation; flatter him at every opportunity (telling him you dreamt about him is always a good chat-up line); and show him what a good listener you are. He loves that in a girl!

If you can't be bothered to do the running . . . he'll pursue you to the max. First, he'll try to impress you with his fancy footwork at the disco. If that doesn't work, he'll write you a song (and sing it to you too if you're "lucky"), send you flowers, and/or inundate you with love letters and other tokens of his affection. And he won't give up until you've at least acknowledged him (and his talents!)

Keep him by . . . analysing his dreams for him; kissing him a lot; having younger siblings or cousins (Piscean blokes love kids); remembering all your silly little anniversaries; not laughing when he sings to you; keeping a straight face when he talks about how you and he were together in a past life.

Dump him when . . . his love letters start making you feel bilious.

Love match: He's capable of loving forever – but only if you're a Cancerian, Virgoan or Scorpian girl.

Top Piscean totty: James Bradfield (Manic Street Preachers), Peter Andre, Jon Bon Jovi, Ronan Keating and Stephen Gately (Boyzone), Evan Dando and Graham Coxon (Blur).

Love Match

Check our specially devised compatibility chart over the page and discover whether or not you and the boy of your dreams are destined to be celestial soul-mates . . .

LOVE MATCH COMPATIBILITY CHART

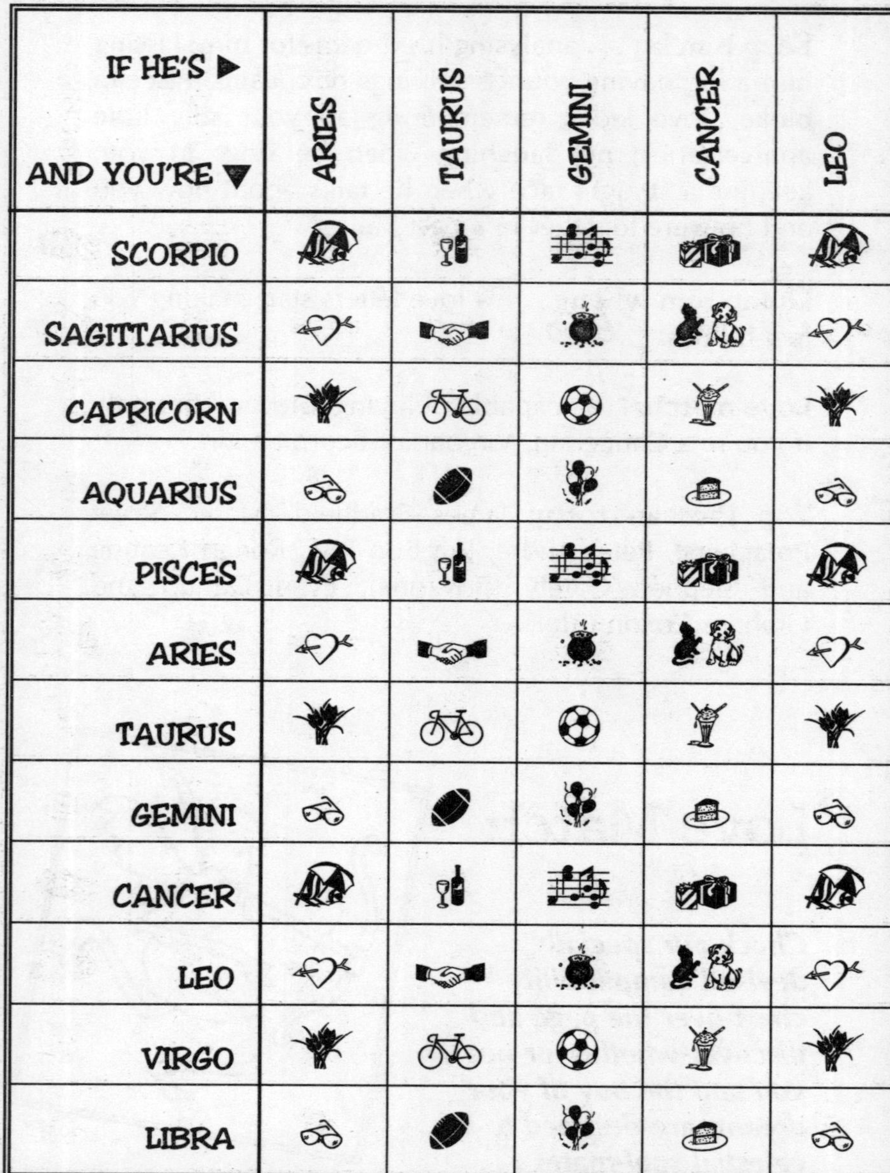

First find your own compatibility symbol,

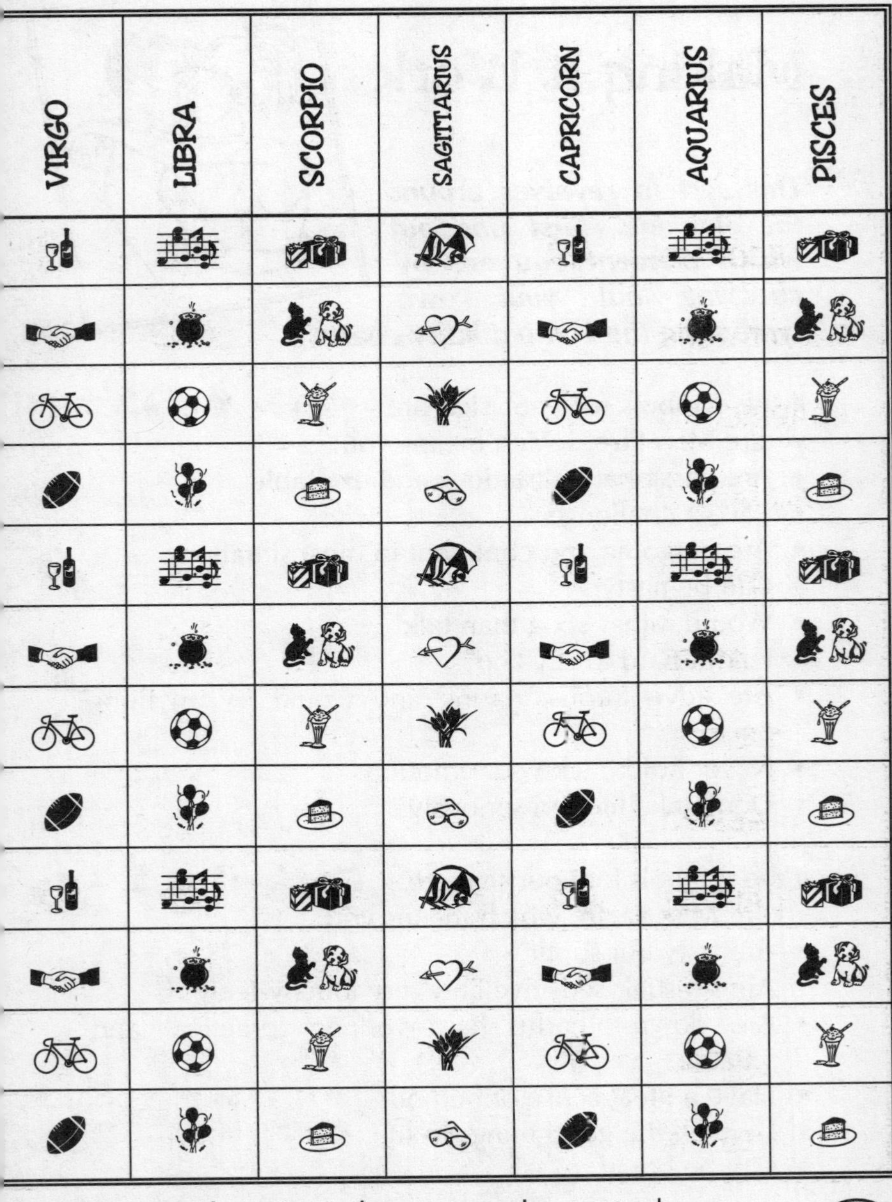

then discover what it says about you and your star boy . . .

Making It Work

This system revolves around the elements. First find out which element you are by checking out your own symbol on the compatibility chart.

If the symbols for your sign are – or – you're **Miss Fire**, which means you:

- Are passionate, flirtatious and excitable
- Love a challenge
- Are outgoing and confident in most situations
- Can be nasty
- Would rather snog than talk!
- Find it hard to say "no"
- Are adventurous, daring and would try anything once
- Never hold back your emotions
- Don't take life too seriously

If the symbols for your sign are – or – you're **Miss Earth**, which means you:

- Are sexy but subtle
- Are sensual, sensitive and very touchy-feely
- Are down-to-earth, hard-working, practical and reliable
- Have a great sense of humour
- Love all the good things in life
- Can be bossy

- Hate anyone saying "no" to you
- Could never be unfaithful
- Take love and life pretty seriously

If the symbols for your sign are – or – you're **Miss Air**, which means you:

- Love a good gossip
- Can be a bit cool
- Have the ability to see people as they really are
- Are always on the phone
- Are childlike and uninhibited.
- Have trouble being faithful in a relationship
- Tend to speak your mind
- Love the thrill of the romantic chase
- Like to be logical, rational and controlled (even when some emotion is called for)

If the symbols for your sign are – or – you're **Miss Water**, which means you:

- Are incredibly romantic
- Are sensitive to the needs, moods and feelings of others
- Need a lot of love, attention and affection
- Can be moody
- Have a fantastic imagination
- Don't mind someone else taking the lead in most situations
- Like art and literature
- Can be talked into doing things you'd rather not do at all
- Are a bit secretive

Now you know which element you are, discover what you can do to make the relationship between you and your chosen bloke a success. Check the symbol for you and your star boy on the compatibility chart, and read on . . .

What a red-hot combination this is! As two fiery Fire signs, this relationship is wild. The main trouble is though that as you're both so lusty, there's no way either of you can contain your desire for passing fancies and are unlikely to be able to stay the course. If either of you decide that you want to get serious, this fiery coupling will burn itself out fairly sharpish. Even if you stay together for the passion, it's unlikely to go on forever: no one (not even someone as passionate as you) can stand *that* much heat!

Make it work by . . .

. . . At least *trying* to stay faithful

. . . Slowing down and realizing that love isn't a race or a competition

. . . Showing your soft side now and again – and that applies to both of you

As a Fire sign, you're a pretty realistic person and although you're enthusiastic when it comes to love, you don't have too many expectations about this

romance. This Earth bloke has both feet firmly planted on the ground and, although you can be steady when you want to be, you may not want to be with *this* bloke, who may prove to be a bit of a drag in the long term. While you're lively and impulsive, he's sedate and cautious and sure to put a damper on any of your bright spark ideas. If you do end up together, then it has a reasonable chance of succeeding, but only if you can keep things interesting.

Make it work by . . .

. . . Making more of an effort to appreciate his sensible side (instead of ridiculing it)

. . . Telling him not to expect you to do all the work – especially when it comes to keeping the relationship alive

. . . Not forcing him to talk when he doesn't want to

His Airy personality may fan your Fire-y one, and although he may have a calming effect on you on one level, it may not make for much excitement. When you first meet, you're likely to be bowled over by his flirtatious charm, and a romance could flare up pretty quickly. He's a bit moody though, and the way he blows hot and cold is perhaps something you may not be able to handle. Generally, he allows you to take the lead and he's happy to do whatever you want, but your demands may prove too much for him in the end.

Make it work by . . .

. . . Being less demanding

. . . Not getting wound up by the things he says and does

. . . Remembering his needs as well as your own

You're Fire; he's Water. You're hot; he's cool. This doesn't mean he's not passionate – he is, but in a very gentle, romantic way. He's fairly traditional by nature and you shock him with your rather forceful personality. And whereas you like romance to be a bit of a laugh, he's deadly serious about it. If you're keen to make a go of this relationship, you may have trouble keeping the fires of passion burning past a certain point. But he's adaptable and willing to learn. And who better to teach him than you?

Make it work by . . .

. . . Appreciating and accepting your differences

. . . Taking him in hand

. . . Helping him look on the bright side of life

If you two get together – and you will because, although you're different in so many ways (you're an Earth sign and he's Fire), you share some basic qualities and interests – what may concern you most is his apparent lack of concern for you. You may look up to him at first, but as your relationship progresses, you realize that he may not be as romantic as you'd initially envisaged him to be. And because you like to be shown a lot of tenderness, this could bother you and could even put you off him. If you can give him the space and inspiration he requires, the flames of passion between you are capable of reaching great heights.

Make it work by . . .

. . . Teaching him how to be more caring
. . . Not placing him on a pedestal
. . . Giving him room to breathe within the relationship

What many might envisage to be a rather safe, possibly unexciting relationship, could easily become a rewarding and emotionally satisfying partnership. You're both Earth signs – gritty, practical and easy to read – and will have an instant liking for each other as soon as you meet. Together, you make a great team, warm and affectionate, each able to help the other free themselves from any insecurities. Because of this, your partnership should succeed.

Make it work by . . .

. . . Not letting others put you off each other
. . . Giving each other almost constant support and encouragement

. . . Not allowing jealousy or possessiveness to come between you

When you first set eyes on him, he's like a breath of fresh air (and he would be – he's an Air sign). You're a solid Earth sign and, to him, represent a port in the storm of life . . . at the start anyway. Although he's charming and extremely sociable, his weird moods may bother you intensely, especially when one minute he's incredibly immature, and the next he's a man of the world. When it comes to love, you know what you like but your lack of spontaneity may bore him. Not that you're boring – far from it – but he needs such constant variety that only a girl with the most powerful imagination and energy could really make him hers. But if you're willing to work at it, it might just turn out OK.

Make it work by . . .

. . . Not expecting the relationship to work without either of you putting in any effort

. . . Being honest about what it is that bugs you both about each other

. . . Dealing with problems as and when they crop up

He needs a girl who's prepared to give him her all, and you may not be ready for all he's asking of you. You're

a realistic Earth sign and alarm bells start ringing for you even on your first date, when all he talks about is love and commitment. You may allow this to wash right over you (he *is* a mega-romantic Water sign, after all), and you find it hard to take such premature romantic rantings seriously. Romantically, he seems so experienced and this is what could make you fall for him. If he starts to believe his somewhat previous words of love, then he could easily fall for you too. This is a relationship that improves with age, so it may well be worth working at.

Make it work by . . .
. . . Making your feelings known at all times
. . . Not throwing it all in at the first sign of trouble
. . . Remembering that he's just as sensitive as you are

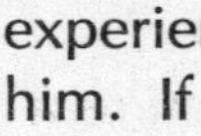

You're a beautiful Airy-fairy and it's hardly surprising that he's initially attracted by your looks. Once he gets to know you, he'll appreciate your wicked sense of humour. He's mesmerized by your ever-changing needs and unpredictable nature, and although this may irritate the hell out of a less challenge-seeking guy, he finds everything about you quite charming. He's a mega-direct Fire sign and you like the way he says what he thinks. You also love his obvious delight in you and his fun-loving, impulsive character. Together, you're constantly changing and, although this could destroy many a relationship, yours will positively thrive on it.

Make it work by . . .
. . . Keeping him entertained
. . . Putting a stop to his constant demands
. . . Not worrying about what other people think

As an Air sign, your head's stuck in the clouds when it comes to love; as an Earth sign, his feet are firmly on the ground. You may not think this pairing could work, but it might . . . mainly because he could just provide you with the stability and security you need (and secretly crave). Having said that, it's unlikely that you fancy him immediately and he may have to prove himself before you'll give him the time of day. He's impressed by your sociable personality (slightly envious too, if the truth be known) and is so proud of you. It's only when you start to feel constrained by his emotional needs and believe your individuality is threatened that you start to panic. This relationship can only work if you make an extra-special effort.

Make it work by . . .
. . . Being more realistic about your relationship
. . . Not expecting so much all the time
. . . Maintaining your independence

Air signs love a chat and when you two Airy types get

together, there's a whole lot of yakking going on! In fact, you talk so much, it's surprising if there's any time left for anything else! You realize pretty quickly how alike you are mentally, and because of this, you may be reluctant to spoil things by getting romantically embroiled. For those who *do* get involved, however, there are surprises that are well worth waiting for. Variety is the spice of your love life and you're both happy to go out of your way to work out new ways of having fun. A good pairing all in all.

Make it work by . . .

. . . Talking less and doing more

. . . Not being scared to admit your feelings for each other

. . . Keeping your romance exciting

You're attracted by his quiet, almost mysterious aura and he's charmed by your easy-going and friendly ways. You both possess a great sense of fun (you especially as a cheeky Air sign) and this is what brings you together ultimately. You're likely to have a great time too, although his regular bouts of insecurity and the fact that you never seem to want to do anything at the same time can bug you at times. His emotions run deep (and they would – he's a Water sign), but in the long term might cause far too many ripples in the relationship for your liking.

Make it work by . . .

. . . Making him feel secure (and that means no more flirting with other boys!)
. . . Getting your body clocks in sync
. . . Not taking responsibility for his happiness

He's a Fire sign and you're attracted to his warm glow, but no matter how hard you try to make him warm to you, you'll soon have him raging. Because you're so different from him, he sees you as a challenge and will do his utmost to ruffle your cool surface. With regards to love and romance, you're quite different, with him being far more passionate than you. If you're one of the more feisty Water signs, you may feel you've met your match, but don't think for a second that you've got any hold over him: he's his own person and if you try to pin him down, the whole thing could get out of control, ending in you getting seriously burnt.

Make it work by . . .

. . . Stopping winding each other up on purpose
. . . Being a bit more laid-back
. . . Looking on the bright side a bit more often

Although you're a Water sign and he's Earth, you're

similar in many ways and are naturally attracted to each other. You may be disappointed to find though, as time goes on, that he can be a bit of a tiresome stick-in-the-mud who doesn't appreciate your impetuous side. Nevertheless, he can provide you with comfort, stability and security; and you can help him to grow in every direction. If you can put up with the way he allows everyday life to interfere with your relationship, and if he can understand that you're not quite as practical as he is, then this relationship might be worth following through.

Make it work by . . .

. . . Understanding that you'll never really see eye to eye on certain matters
. . . Appreciating his bad points
. . . Letting him know when you're upset

His charm captivates you, but you can't understand why he finds it so hard to have eyes only for you. As a restless Air sign, he wants constant variety, and this may be a whim you're disinclined to entertain. In your opinion, he's a bit mad and, although you may find this exciting at first, you'll soon be wondering when he's going to start behaving "normally". Chances are, he won't. And when he realizes that as a commitment-keen Water sign you're after more than just a good time, he might fly off.

Make it work by . . .

. . . Not trying to change him

. . . Chilling out a bit

. . . Not swamping him with emotional demands

As two Water signs, your thoughts and feelings flow together naturally, and in theory you should get on fine. You both like to take the lead in love, but because you're both so sensitive, problems could arise. You're also both very possessive – him more so – and jealousy could cause many rows. On the up side, he can make you feel desirable and he feels you really understand him; if you want to make a go of it, you could form a very deep bond. But it won't be easy, that's for certain . . .

Make it work by . . .

. . . Taking it in turns to be boss

. . . Talking through any worries you have about your relationship

. . . Really *wanting* it to work

The Venus Effect

Discover where love planet Venus was on the day you were born and your romantic personality will be revealed . . .

Look to the list below to find out which sign Venus was in on your birth day . . .

Birth date	***Venus was in . . .***
1979	
Jan 1–6	Scorpio
Jan 7–Feb 4	Sagittarius
Feb 5–Mar 3	Capricorn
Mar 4–28	Aquarius
Mar 29–Apr 22	Pisces
Apr 23–May 17	Aries
May 18–Jun 11	Taurus
Jun 12–Jul 5	Gemini
Jul 6–31	Cancer
Aug 1–23	Leo
Aug 24–Sep 16	Virgo
Sep 17–Oct 10	Libra
Oct 11–Nov 3	Scorpio
Nov 4–28	Sagittarius
Nov 29–Dec 22	Capricorn
Dec 23–31	Aquarius

Birth date	***Venus was in . . .***
1980	
Jan 1–15	Aquarius
Jan 16–Feb 9	Pisces
Feb 10–Mar 6	Aries
Mar 7–Apr 3	Taurus
Apr 4–May 12	Gemini
May 13–Jun 4	Cancer
Jun 5–Aug 6	Gemini
Aug 7–Sep 7	Cancer
Sep 8–Oct 4	Leo
Oct 5–29	Virgo
Oct 30–Nov 23	Libra
Nov 24–Dec 17	Scorpio
Dec 18–31	Sagittarius
1981	
Jan 1–10	Sagittarius
Jan 11–Feb 3	Capricorn
Feb 4–27	Aquarius
Feb 28–Mar 23	Pisces
Mar 24–Apr 17	Aries
Apr 18–May 11	Taurus
May 12–Jun 4	Gemini
Jun 5–29	Cancer
Jun 30–Jul 24	Leo
Jul 25–Aug 18	Virgo
Aug 19–Sep 12	Libra
Sep 13–Oct 8	Scorpio
Oct 9–Nov 5	Sagittarius
Nov 6–Dec 8	Capricorn
Dec 9–31	Aquarius

Birth date	*Venus was in . . .*
1982	
Jan 1–22	Aquarius
Jan 23–Mar 1	Capricorn
Mar 2–Apr 6	Aquarius
Apr 7–May 4	Pisces
May 5–30	Aries
May 31–Jun 25	Taurus
Jun 26–Jul 20	Gemini
Jul 21–Aug 13	Cancer
Aug 14–Sep 7	Leo
Sep 8–Oct 1	Virgo
Oct 2–25	Libra
Oct 26–Nov 18	Scorpio
Nov 19–Dec 12	Sagittarius
Dec 13–31	Capricorn
1983	
Jan 1–5	Capricorn
Jan 6–29	Aquarius
Jan 30–Feb 22	Pisces
Feb 23–Mar 18	Aries
Mar 19–Apr 12	Taurus
Apr 13–May 8	Gemini
May 9–Jun 5	Cancer
Jun 6–Jul 9	Leo
Jul 10–Aug 26	Virgo
Aug 27–Oct 5	Leo
Oct 6–Nov 8	Virgo
Nov 9–Dec 6	Libra
Dec 7–31	Scorpio

Birth date	***Venus was in . . .***
1984	
Jan 1–25	Sagittarius
Jan 26–Feb 18	Capricorn
Feb 19–Mar 14	Aquarius
Mar 15–Apr 7	Pisces
Apr 8–May 1	Aries
May 2–26	Taurus
May 27–Jun 19	Gemini
Jun 20–Jul 13	Cancer
Jul 14–Aug 7	Leo
Aug 8–31	Virgo
Sep 1–25	Libra
Sep 26–Oct 19	Scorpio
Oct 20–Nov 13	Sagittarius
Nov 14–Dec 8	Capricorn
Dec 9–31	Aquarius
1985	
Jan 1–3	Aquarius
Jan 4–Feb 1	Pisces
Feb 2–Jun 5	Aries
Jun 6–Jul 5	Taurus
Jul 6–Aug 1	Gemini
Aug 2–28	Cancer
Aug 29–Sep 21	Leo
Sep 22–Oct 16	Virgo
Oct 17–Nov 9	Libra
Nov 10–Dec 3	Scorpio
Dec 4–26	Sagittarius
Dec 27–31	Capricorn

Birth date	***Venus was in . . .***
1986	
Jan 1–19	Capricorn
Jan 20–Feb 12	Aquarius
Feb 13–Mar 8	Pisces
Mar 9–Apr 1	Aries
Apr 2–26	Taurus
Apr 27–May 21	Gemini
May 22–Jun 15	Cancer
Jun 16–Jul 11	Leo
Jul 12–Aug 7	Virgo
Aug 8–Sep 6	Libra
Sep 7–Dec 31	Scorpio
1987	
Jan 1–6	Scorpio
Jan 7–Feb 4	Sagittarius
Feb 5–Mar 2	Capricorn
Mar 3–28	Aquarius
Mar 29–Apr 22	Pisces
Apr 23–May 16	Aries
May 17–Jun 10	Taurus
Jun 11–Jul 6	Gemini
Jul 7–29	Cancer
Jul 30–Aug 23	Leo
Aug 24–Sep 16	Virgo
Sep 17–Oct 10	Libra
Oct 11–Nov 3	Scorpio
Nov 4–27	Sagittarius
Nov 28–Dec 21	Capricorn
Dec 22–31	Aquarius

Birth date	***Venus was in . . .***
1988	
Jan 1–15	Aquarius
Jan 16–Feb 9	Pisces
Feb 10–Mar 5	Aries
Mar 6–Apr 3	Taurus
Apr 4–May 17	Gemini
May 18–26	Cancer
May 27–Aug 6	Gemini
Aug 7–Sep 6	Cancer
Sep 7–Oct 4	Leo
Oct 5–29	Virgo
Oct 30–Nov 23	Libra
Nov 24–Dec 17	Scorpio
Dec 18–31	Sagittarius
1989	
Jan 1–10	Sagittarius
Jan 11–Feb 3	Capricorn
Feb 4–27	Aquarius
Feb 28–Mar 23	Pisces
Mar 24–Apr 16	Aries
Apr 17–May 10	Taurus
May 11–Jun 4	Gemini
Jun 5–28	Cancer
Jun 29–Jul 23	Leo
Jul 24–Aug 17	Virgo
Aug 18–Sep 12	Libra
Sep 13–Oct 8	Scorpio
Oct 9–Nov 4	Sagittarius
Nov 5–Dec 9	Capricorn
Dec 10–31	Aquarius

Venus In Aries

Ups:

- You have a warm, loving nature
- You're always attractive to the opposite sex
- You have no fear about telling a boy if you fancy him
- You bring a lot of laughter into any relationship

Downs:

- You sometimes start rows just for the sheer hell of it
- You're not too good at choosing boyfriends, often ending up with someone totally unsuitable
- You don't find it easy to express your feelings
- You can be selfish

Venus In Taurus

Ups:

- Your love life is uncomplicated
- You're good-looking and charming
- You're affectionate and attentive
- You're sensual, considerate and faithful

Downs:

- Your tendency to be over-possessive and jealous can cause problems
- You can easily get into a romantic rut
- You have the potential to "waste" your love on someone quite undeserving
- You've got a fierce temper if you don't get what you want

Venus In Gemini

Ups:

- Guys can't get enough of you!
- You're ace at flirting
- You're really exciting company
- When love wanes, you find it easy to bounce back

Downs:

- You're easily bored and can end a potentially great romance because of that
- Your need to have two or three relationships simultaneously can get you into trouble
- You need constant mental stimulation (and, sadly, not many boys can provide that)
- You don't take other people's feelings seriously enough

Venus In Cancer

Ups:

- You're loyal, loving and lovable
- Your ever-changing moods make you very interesting company
- When you get the right sort of attention, you blossom into one of the sexiest girls around
- You always mean what you say – even though you don't always say what you mean . . .

Downs:

- You're a slave to your emotions
- You're a bit unrealistic about love
- You're too trusting at times

- You're so scared of being hurt, you'll avoid getting too close to anyone

Venus In Leo

Ups:

- You always stand out from the crowd
- You enjoy the whole process of forming relationships and love being in love
- You're generous, faithful and warm-hearted.
- You have the ability to make a boyfriend feel really special

Downs:

- You're so keen to be in a relationship, you rather rush into things and make loads of romantic mistakes
- Your sense of judgment isn't all that it should be
- You suffer more than your fair share of heartache
- You need loads of attention and don't always get it

Venus In Virgo

Ups:

- You are emotionally generous, always eager to please the one you love
- You're caring and thoughtful
- You're an exciting mixture of homely and sexy
- Because you're so intelligent and level-headed, you don't make too many mistakes on the love front

Downs:
- You can be inhibited
- You can be a bit of a mother hen with your boyfriend
- Your fussiness means you can go for long periods boyfriend-free
- You're all too easily put off by things that really don't matter

Venus In Libra

Ups:
- You're fun-loving and attractive
- You're extremely popular with the opposite sex and have no trouble charming the ones you fancy into submission
- You're sympathetic and fair-minded
- You always stay great mates with your exes

Downs:
- Your fear of hurting anyone's feelings means that you're just a girl who can't say no – and this gets you into all sorts of tricky situations
- Your love life is likely to be complicated
- Quite often, you fall in love just because you're in that sort of mood – and who the object of your affections might be is almost irrelevant
- You'd rather be with *anyone* than be alone

Venus In Scorpio

Ups:
- You can cope with any problems love throws at you

- You're passionate, intense and quite unforgettable
- When in love, you're incredibly loyal
- You're very sexy

Downs:

- You take love and life too seriously sometimes
- You often go for unavailable types
- Because of your obsessive tendencies, you run the risk of developing major, destination-nowhere crushes
- When a relationship ends, you can get nasty, particularly if you feel you've been wronged

Venus In Sagittarius

Ups:

- With your fantastic sense of humour and free-thinking ways, you're attractive to many members of the opposite sex
- In a relationship, you will enthral your partner with your fun-loving ways
- You're caring, warm and affectionate
- You're enthusiastic, energetic and communicative

Downs:

- As a naturally friendly and frank person, your openness is often taken the wrong way
- You need tons of freedom – something only a few boyfriends will be able to give you
- Your unpredictable behaviour baffles many a potential boyfriend
- You see love as some sort of game – and this can cause problems

Venus In Capricorn

Ups:

- You're persistent and always get your man, no matter how long it takes
- You have a talent for choosing great boyfriends
- You're faithful, loving and loyal
- Your great sense of humour makes you very attractive

Downs:

- You can be too cool sometimes, causing boys to see you as aloof and stand-offish
- You don't allow yourself to get deep enough into relationships to feel comfortable about expressing yourself
- Your great sense of logic often holds you back from getting involved in the first place
- Flirting doesn't come easy to you

Venus In Aquarius

Ups:

- You're physically very attractive and unquestionably cool
- You are always surrounded by admirers – even though you may be completely oblivious to them
- You're never short of potential boyfriends
- When you find someone who shares your outlook and understands your need for independence, you're an interesting and loyal partner

Downs:

- You can't differentiate between friendship and love and sometimes go out with someone who would have been best kept as a friend
- You fall in love far too easily
- You often make the mistake of trying to "change" boyfriends and most of them don't take kindly to this
- You tend to like a boy for what he *could* be rather than for what he is

Venus In Pisces

Ups:

- You're one of the most romantic signs of the zodiac
- You write the best love letters and have even been known to pen the odd love poem!
- You're attractive, compassionate and sensitive
- There's a queue of lads waiting to go out with you!

Downs:

- You have problems with jealousy, arising from your own insecurities
- You find it hard ending a relationship, even when you know it's not working
- You're waiting for Mr Perfect and don't seem to realize that he may not exist
- You make far too many sacrifices for boyfriends who don't deserve it

Part 4:

Friends And Rivals

Are You A Great Mate?

Yes, but not to just anyone . . . As a Scorpio, it's unlikely that you'll have that many close mates – not because you're unpopular, but because you're so fussy. When you do get close to someone, you like to get really close and can be fairly possessive. You're constant with it though – and would never drop a friend without a really good reason. When a mate's good to you, you'll be ace in return – very generous, happy to offer advice and always ready to provide a shoulder to cry on. Of all the signs of the zodiac, you're the least likely to gossip, which makes you a bit restrained when it comes to a good old girlie sesh, but extremely trustworthy!

You make friends because you're:

- Absolutely hilarious
- Really generous
- Always able to make people feel welcome (even when they call round at the worst possible moment!)
- Not gossipy in the slightest: you can be entrusted with the juiciest morsels and they'll go no further
- Reliable
- Totally trustworthy: any secret you're told is safe forever

You lose friends because you're:

- Lazy about getting in touch
- Even lazier about answering the phone (especially if you've got an answerphone to do it for you)
- Able to read people's minds
- Liable to turn nasty if you're upset
- Unnecessarily suspicious of everyone's actions and motives
- Just plain spiteful sometimes

Who's Your Friend?

You have specific requirements when it comes to playmates: they should be interesting *and* interested (in you preferably) without being too demanding. You like to have common interests with your mates, and enjoy "playing" with them and sharing these interests. Many Scorpians meet mates through sports they enjoy and will spend as much time as possible with friends who enjoy the same activities. You need friends who really understand you and your moods: when you're feeling down, they should be able to cheer you up and encourage you to discuss your worries. (You're always bottling up your feelings.) And your best mates, who are all too aware of how jealous you can be, won't compete with you in any way or do anything to make you envious of them. Your fave friends are exceptionally loyal – that's why you should hang out with Cancerians and Pisceans (both Water signs who share many of your qualities and interests), Virgoans (who won't be your best mate, but will be there when you need them), Taureans (who aren't much like you, but are great pals nonetheless) and Capricorns (who are loyal to the max!) Because you're a fast-thinking, quick-talking, deep-thinking person, who really hasn't got any time for people who can't keep up with you or who are too unlike you, you're unlikely to get friendly with showy Ariens and Leos, superficial Librans or loud and lairy Sagittarians.

Your Best Mate . . .

. . . is the type of person who would:

- Drop everything to play a game of pool with you (and let you win!)
- Bring you your fave choccie bar when you're feeling miserable
- Talk through your problems with you without making you feel that they're prying
- Never go out with a bloke you fancied (no matter how much she fancied him herself)
- Never let you down
- Not dream of flaunting something they've got and know you'd like

The Other Signs As Friends

You've read all about what makes a Scorpian friend. But what about the other eleven signs? Here's a list of their good and bad qualities . . .

Sagittarians . . .

. . . make great mates because they're:

- Sociable
- Always willing to stick up for their mates (even if they don't really agree with them)
- Honest
- Open-minded

. . . are dead-end friends because they're:

- *Too* honest sometimes (some would call it totally tactless)
- Prone to temper tantrums
- Occasionally violent and abusive – verbally and physically
- Unable to keep a secret

Capricornians . . .

. . . make great mates because they're:

- Happy to stick by their nearest and dearest through thick and thin
- Sincere

- Wildly generous when it comes to their mates' birthdays
- Ever so kind (when they want to be)

. . . are dead-end friends because they're:

- Terrible judges of character
- Quite vicious if they're rejected in any way
- Unnecessarily suspicious of everyone and sometimes test their friends – just to see how loyal they are
- Users – or are capable of using a mate to get something (or someone) they want

Aquarians . . .

. . . make great mates because they're:

- Intelligent and interesting
- Happy to make a lot of effort when it comes to staying in touch with friends
- Not bothered about being woken up at four in the morning to help a friend in need (most of the time anyway . . .)
- Majorly friendly and sociable

. . . are dead-end friends because they're:

- Inclined to want everyone – mates especially – to live by their own rather high standards
- Always stealing your ideas
- Desperate to be the boss in all relationships
- Occasionally self-centred, in that sometimes they believe their problems are more important than anyone else's

Pisceans . . .

. . . make great mates because they're:

- Unbiased and unprejudiced
- Always willing to listen
- A real laugh
- Happy to do all the organizing when it comes to nights out (even though they're not very good at it. Aw, shame . . .)

. . . are dead-end friends because they're:

- A bit disorganized and forgetful
- Very insecure
- Occasionally cold and offhand for no real reason
- Mad as snakes!

Ariens . . .

. . . make great mates because they're:

- Warm
- Broadminded
- Generous
- Entertaining

. . . are dead-end friends because they're:

- Selfish
- Often inconsiderate
- Competitive
- Impatient

Taureans . . .

. . . make great mates because they're:

- Affectionate

- Reliable
- Strong
- Trustworthy

... are dead-end friends because they're:

- Possessive
- A bit dismissive of any form of weakness
- Tactless
- Snobby

Geminians ...

... make great mates because they're:

- Spontaneous
- Helpful
- Tons of fun
- Amusing

... are dead-end friends because they're:

- Never on time
- Prone to fibbing
- Fickle
- Unpredictable

Cancerians ...

... make great mates because they're:

- Kind
- Hospitable
- Sensitive
- Loyal

... are dead-end friends because they're:

- Hypersensitive

- Prone to bearing grudges – for ages!
- Judgmental
- Clingy

Leos . . .

. . . make great mates because they're:

- Great fun
- Generous
- Proud of you
- Loving

. . . are dead-end friends because they're:

- Easily upset
- Likely to ignore you for no apparent reason
- Hard to get to know properly
- A bit pig-headed

Virgoans . . .

. . . make great mates because they're:

- Fussy about who they're friends with. (If you're a Virgoan's mate, count yourself privileged!)
- Refined
- Considerate
- Keen to help in any way they can

. . . are dead-end friends because they're:

- Hypercritical
- Terrible worriers
- A bit sarky sometimes
- Always right (or *think* they are anyway . . .)

Librans . . .

. . . make great mates because they're:

- Loving and lovable
- Honest
- Fair
- Gentle

. . . are dead-end friends because they're:
- *Sooo* indecisive
- Occasionally jealous (especially of mates who are prettier than them)
- A bit grumpy sometimes
- Very sulky (especially if you neglect them for any period of time)

Forever Friends?

Now you've got the general idea of what all the separate signs are like, check the friendship chart over the page to find out more about friendship compatibility . . .

There's an astrological theory about friendship which revolves around the order of the signs. To discover how it works, take a look at the chart on the next page, find your sign down the side and your friends' signs along the top, make a note of the symbol where the two signs meet, then check the "key" panel below. This should give you a good indication of how you and your mates get on . . .

Friendship Chart

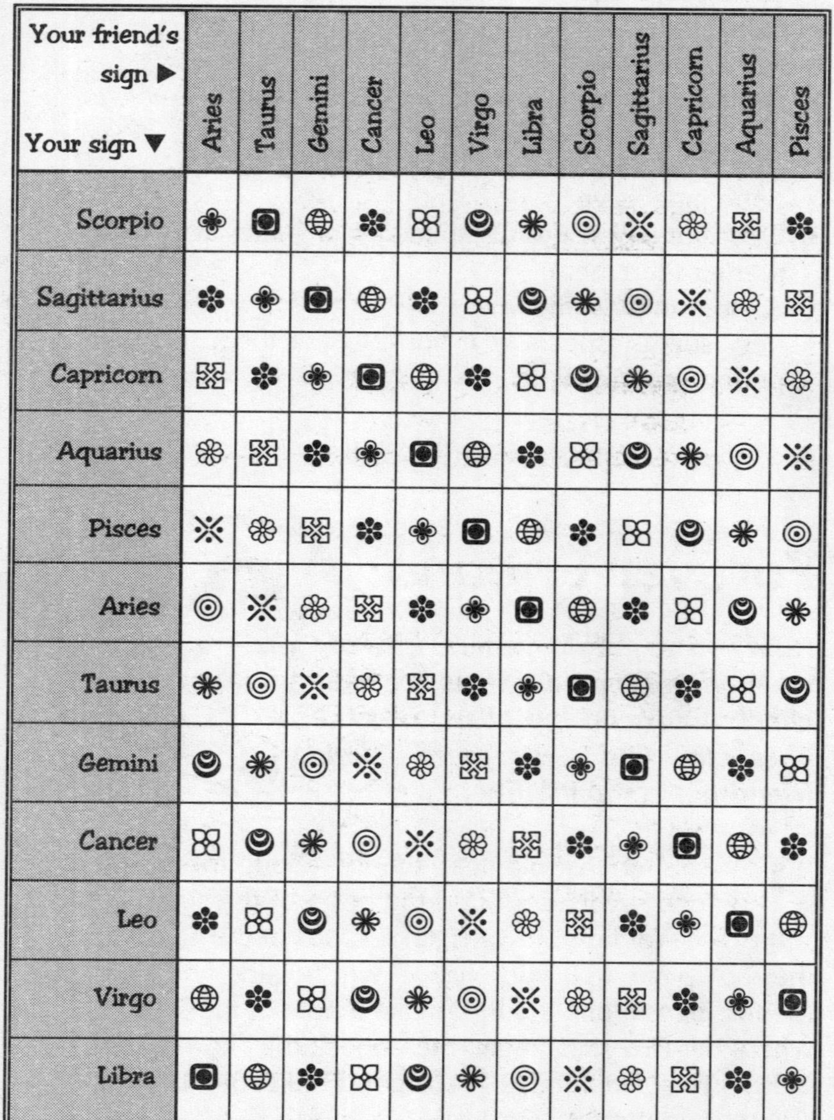

Key:

◎ – If you and a friend are the same sign – Scorpio in this instance – you're too similar. You can be friends, but because you're so aware of each other's failings, you're likely to drive each other mad and need to be extra tolerant.

❃ – If you make friends with a person who is one sign ahead of you – as a Scorpian, this would be a Sagittarian – they're very different from you, but are in possession of many of the qualities that you aspire to have. This person is a real example to you, is able to teach you many things (if you're prepared to learn, that is), and can lead you from where you are now in life to the next stage. But, because of your obvious differences, you're unlikely to be best mates.

※ – A friend whose sign is the one before yours – Libra in your case – may appear to be radically different from you on the surface, but has a great understanding of your innermost fears and desires. They're a good person to fall back on in times of trouble, as they can listen without being judgmental. But, if you go out socializing together, you're unlikely to have that great a time. (That's if you can even agree on where you are going to go and what you are going to do in the first place!)

◉ – Someone two signs ahead of you – and for you, as a Scorpio, this would be a Capricorn – is a person you're really comfortable with. This person is almost like a brother or sister to you: you're able to spend a lot of time in their company (in fact, many friends two signs apart can even live together quite happily), but this relationship won't be as exciting as others you might have. This mate is mega-loyal though, will always be there for you, so is well worth hanging on to.

– A friend whose sign is two signs behind yours – a Virgo in your case – is capable of being a great mate. You may not have an overwhelming need to see a lot of each other, but when you do you're sure to have a fine time. It's unlikely that you'll ever get *really* close to this person, but stick with them and they'll prove what a good friend they can be time and time again.

– If your friend is three signs ahead of you – and as a Scorpio, that would make them an Aquarius – you could find them rather difficult. Not difficult enough to put you off wanting to spend time with them, but more of a challenge. You have differing views on almost everything, but this just makes for plenty of heated debate. Occasionally, this person really gets on your nerves, but for the most part you find them *kind* of entertaining.

– If you have a friend whose sign is three signs behind yours – a mate who's a Leo in your case, Miss Scorpio – you may not be on the most intimate terms, but they often feel obliged to help you. You don't have an emotional or spiritual link with this person, but may see eye to eye on other matters – work, maybe; money, perhaps. They're the sort of friend you can rely on for sensible advice and are able to point you in the right direction on a practical level. But they have to be in the right frame of mind to do it . . .

✿ – If you've befriended an individual who is four signs ahead of you **or** four signs behind you – a Pisces or a Cancer in your case – you share the same element (Water, in this case) and are likely to have tons in common. Sometimes, you can feel envious of them, especially the friend who is four signs ahead of you (Pisces) and you may long to be as talented as they are. On the other hand, they can be a real inspiration to you, firing your ambitions and giving you lots of ideas, but if you spend too much time together, the envy could get the better of you in the end . . .

🌐 – A friend who's five signs ahead of you – and for you, Scorpio, that would be an Aries – is *capable* of helping you get to where you want to be, but may not *want* to help you. Not much of a mate at all really . . .

❀ – Someone five signs behind you – a Gemini in your case – is so very alien to you, but there's something about them that you find interesting. It's not that you have anything in common with this person – you're like chalk and cheese – but you have a strange kind of respect for the way they run their life. Even though you don't understand much of their behaviour, for some reason you just can't help being mesmerized by them. Weird, or what?

■ – Your opposite sign – the sign that's six signs ahead of or behind your own (Taurus in your case) – will be naturally attracted to you and, to start with, you may believe that you have a lot in common. On the surface it seems that way, but once you get to know each other you realize just how different you are. This can lead to conflict but more often than not it makes for an exciting (though unpredictable) friendship. You are different on every level – physical, intellectual and emotional – and, while this can be a pain sometimes, ultimately you seem to complement each other and get on just fine.

With Friends Like That . . .

Some signs of the zodiac really don't get on with other signs – not one little bit. Read on to discover who's who in the world of rivals . . .

As a Scorpian, you're sometimes a tad paranoid and need trustworthy types as mates; that's why rowdy **Ariens** and blabbermouth **Aquarians** wouldn't do as friends for you at all. It's a shame, because those two signs are really quite fond of you. In fact, you'd be seriously surprised to discover who'd be most likely to hide sardines in your curtain pole: it'd be none other than a crazy **Gemini** or a mad **Leo**. Who'd have thought it, eh?

And the other signs?

Sagittarius

Sagittarians like a laugh so wouldn't be seen dead with a stick-in-the-mud **Taurean** or a moochy old **Piscean** (Saggie's opinion only). A Sagittarian would be more inclined to seek out the company of a **Cancerian** or a **Virgoan**, which is a shame because *they'd* probably turn Saggie down, due to the fact that they find them really annoying . . . Sad but true.

Capricorn

Capricornians need friends, but they will not tolerate **Ariens** or **Geminians** under any circumstances. Not that these signs would cause them any harm – as you know, Aries and Gemini types don't actually pay too much attention to Capricorns at all. The people Capricornians should steer well clear of – and who could, if they wanted to, do untold damage to a Capricorn's reputation – are **Leos** (who find Caps immensely dull) and **Librans** (who won't even spare them the time of day).

Aquarius

Aquarians like excitement but, in their opinion, that's not something they'll get from ploddy old **Taureans** and depressing old **Cancerians**. Not that these folk are particularly nasty to Aquarius. Oh no. Real enemies come in the guise of vicious (and they *can* be when the mood takes them) **Virgoans** and you spiteful **Scorpians**: you're the ones who'll plant cress seeds in their carpet and water it while they're on holiday . . .

Pisces

Pisceans like a laugh; so do **Leos**. The trouble is, neither sign is that funny (not in each other's opinion anyway), so laughs would be seriously lacking if they ever got together. Pisceans often find themselves mildly amused by **Geminians**, but once within twenty paces of each other, rubbing up the wrong way begins. But the people Pisceans should really make an effort to avoid are **Librans** and **Sagittarians** – they aren't normally nasty, but they just can't resist bullying a Piscean.

Aries

Ariens may have a lot of mates but, if the truth be known, they don't actually like many people at all. Which is strange because, all in all, they're pretty popular themselves. The people they dislike most tend to be fellow **Ariens**, **Cancerians** and **Virgoans**. If they get hate mail, it *may* be from an Arien, but it's more likely to be sent by one of you **Scorpians** or a **Capricornian** – you lot aren't keen on rams at all.

Taurus

Taureans are likeable sorts, and would have you believe that they are incapable of being nasty. But, deep down, they're just as capable as anyone else of upsetting people and making enemies. The sign that bugs a Taurean the most however is **Leo** – they just *can't* get on; and, although **Librans** are ruled by the same planet as Taurus (Venus), that's about all they've got in common. They're unlikely to receive hate mail from these people though – mainly because it's **Sagittarians** and **Aquarians** who are Taurus' worst enemies . . . They just don't understand Taureans at all and that worries them silly.

Gemini

Geminians are friendly and give most people the benefit of the doubt. Everybody except virtuous **Virgoans** that is, who, although ruled by planet Mercury (the same planet that rules Gemini), are a right royal pain in the butt to slightly immoral Gemini! You **Scorpio** folk aren't too popular with Geminians either: you're just *soooo* infuriating! (In Gemini's opinion anyway.) But any poison pen letters that land on a Geminian's doormat are most likely to have been sent by a **Capricornian** (who finds Gemini's ways immensely aggravating) or a **Piscean** (who could be just plain jealous).

Cancer

Cancerians sometimes seem to hate everyone – they get *that* grumpy! The people they consistently dislike are **Librans** and **Sagittarians**. Librans are so blimmin' wishy-washy (in Cancer's opinion) and Sagittarians don't seem to have anything in common with Cancer at all. Which is strange, because Libra and Sagittarius don't have too many problems with Cancer. But it's **Aquarians** and **Ariens** who find Cancerians the most bugsome. Such is life, eh?

Leo

Leos aren't overly keen on **Scorpians** (for a myriad of

reasons) and **Capricornians** (who seem only to be friendly to Leo when they want something). In return though, Scorpio tries to lean on Leo on occasion and Capricorn kind of looks up to them, but that doesn't really interest Leo. Real rivals aren't you folk at all though: Leos should watch out for **Taureans** and **Pisceans** – they're the ones out to get 'em! Yikes!

Virgo

Virgoans are right old fusspots and, because they're so picky when it comes to mates, should sometimes count themselves lucky to have any mates at all! The people who peeve them the most are **Sagittarians** and **Aquarians**: Virgo has no use for them at all. But real enemies come in the form of **Ariens** and **Geminians** – they've *really* got it in for Virgo.

Libra

Librans are real sweethearts but that doesn't stop them disliking people from time to time. They're generally patient types but can, on occasion, get irritated. Top offenders, in Libra's eyes, are **Capricornians** and **Pisceans** – they're such a pain! But if anyone's going to boil a Libran's bunny, it'll be a **Taurean** or a **Cancerian**. They might *seem* soft, but when they get riled, they get *really* riled. (And sometimes all it takes is a Libran getting in their way.)

Part 5:

Home And Family

Scorpio At Home

Let's be honest, you're not the easiest member of the zodiac to live with. You require privacy, quiet and your own personal space – not always possible, especially if you have brothers and sisters.

Your Room

In an ideal world, your room would look out onto a beautiful lake or stunning waterfall – something of a contradiction considering Scorpios are thought to be natural city dwellers. Whatever the size of your room, one thing's for sure – you'll have "customized" it to look like yours and no one else's. You need a sanctuary where you feel you can shut out the world, play your fave sounds and be yourself. You like a bit of luxury so it's likely your room will have a distinctly "expensive" feel to it. You're willing to save up or badger your folks to get you something you really want.

You like a dramatic, striking style of decor. The walls of your room are probably painted in rich, dark shades – midnight blue, crimson, burgundy, bottle green, perhaps even charcoal grey or black. Your choice of lighting adds to this exotic look. You demand subtlety and you're the queen of the dimmer switch! When it comes to fabrics, apart from leather and PVC, you're into rich velvets, sensuous silks and seductive satins, all in your favourite dark colours.

Flowers are important to you, especially hothouse blooms like orchids. Your love of the exotic will also be apparent from your choice of "knick-knacks". No collection of cutesy china animals for you – you're far more likely have an unusual sculpture or array of peacock feathers – and you just *love* mirrors. You adorn your walls with paintings and pictures depicting scenes of heat and passion – flamenco dancers for instance – and posters of your favourite bands.

Happy Families?

Your family is very important to you but as you have a strong need for your own space, there could be problems if your parents don't really understand this. The star signs of individual family members have great bearing on how you get on. There's an astrological theory that if you're one of the "masculine" signs (i.e. Aries, Gemini, Leo, Libra, Sagittarius or Aquarius), you'll be most influenced throughout your childhood by your dad; and if your star sign is "feminine" (Taurus, Cancer, Virgo, Scorpio, Capricorn or Pisces), then you're more likely to be influenced by your mum. As a Scorpio, you'll probably find it's your mum who exerts the most power over you.

You And Your Parents*

Scorpians have intense feelings, which they usually prefer to keep to themselves – and this makes it difficult for mums and dads to help if something's troubling their Scorpio kid. Parents will also disapprove of the way you are able to fib so easily. But no matter how incompatible you may be with your Ma and/or Pa, they'll certainly be aware of – and, more often than not, admire – your tremendous willpower and determination.

You'll love your **Arien** mum or dad's youthful attitude to life. But sometimes Aries dad really annoys you by being too impulsive, while Aries mum's hot temper tends to ignite your own.

You'll love your **Taurean** mum because she's patient and loving but her innate stubbornness may drive you barmy. Taurus dad is a sweetie – the perfect pop for you, in fact! – even if he is a bit slow to catch on at times.

You may be impressed by a **Geminian** parent's sparkling, ready wit but Gemini mum can be so nosy and Gemini dad is the ultimate dad from hell for a Scorpian. He's so sociable, he can't understand why you like spending time alone.

Cancerian mum *tries* to be understanding and sympathetic but she's so over-protective, there'll be times when she'll feel like a noose around your neck.

*If you don't live with your parents, consider the star signs of your guardian/s or main carer/s instead.

Cancer dad respects your need for privacy more, but at times you think he's really lazy.

Leos, even when they're parents, can't help showing off and there are probably times when you wish they were more grown-up and dignified.

On the whole, you get on with a **Virgoan** mum or dad. Like you, they're hardworking and intelligent. You differ in that Virgos tend not to understand your deeply intense feelings. And that could cause rifts.

You've probably got a sign on your door saying "Keep Out" if you've a **Libran** mum. She just doesn't understand your need for privacy. But Libra dad has enough charm to wheedle his way into your confidence.

You'll understand a **Scorpian** parent well – a Scorpio mum in particular. They respect your desire for space, and understand your need to be secretive. Why – they'll even let you have a lock for your bedroom door!

You probably don't have that much in common with a **Sagittarian** parent. Your Sag dad may accuse you of being rude when you refuse to join him on one of his walks but you will appreciate Sag mum's intelligence.

Ambitious **Capricornian** dad's just the man to spur you on to better things. Capricorn mum is just as supportive but possibly a tad too bossy for your liking.

Aquarian folk are famous for being tolerant – always a prized quality in a parent – but they're maybe a little too unconventional for you. You're a straight-down-the line type and want your parents to act like parents.

Piscean dad is your kind of dad – he's sensitive and understands your moods. You'll adore Pisces mum too: she's incredibly intuitive and is willing to devote limitless time and energy to you.

Any Brothers Or Sisters?

Not being particularly sociable, Scorpios don't usually mind being only children. If you're part of a big family, you may become very close to one brother or sister in particular. You're prone to jealousy and may not be able to help feeling jealous of a sibling. So which star sign suits Scorpio best as a sister or brother?

Like you, **Arien siblings** are competitive and like to work hard. However, they don't have your determination or willpower and arguments may occur when you come out on top.

A **Taurean sister** or **brother** is so friendly and well-meaning, they won't feel like much of a threat to you. You'll enjoy gently teasing younger siblings but the stubbornness of older ones may well annoy you.

It's doubtful you'll have a serene home life if you have **Geminian siblings**, particularly if you have to share a room. Gemini brothers? Just be grateful they're not sisters!

Fellow Water Signs, **Cancerian brothers** and **sisters** are usually your kind of people. However an older Cancer sister may mother you while you may slightly intimidate a shy, younger Cancer brother.

Leo siblings, with their constant showing off, can be a pain in the neck – a tad annoying when you want to be the centre of attention.

You're on the same wavelength as a **Virgoan brother** or **sister**. However, Virgos can be critical and you won't take kindly to being told off by them.

You'll get on with an easy-going **Libran sibling** to a certain extent but basically you're very different. A Libran brother may gently tease you. As for a Libra sister? How come she never gets worked up about things that drive you insane?

A **Scorpian sibling** will respect your desire for privacy, understand how you feel and be just as determined as you. Scorpio brothers are ace, with their off-the-wall sense of humour, but you may be a teensy bit jealous of a Scorpio sister.

Sagittarians make great siblings. They're sociable but not too intrusive, and very tolerant. You'll get on with a **Sag bro** but a **Sag sis** is probably the best a Scorpio can possibly have. She's never jealous, is a good listener and can laugh you out of a mood.

You generally like **Capricornians**. They're resolute, hardworking and ambitious. Your Capricorn brother is A-plus where you're concerned because he's all of the above *and* he's practical. The ideal confidante.

Aquarian brother or **sister** and you? Mmm, not the best combination. They tend to annoy you because they hold such wishy-washy, airy-fairy views on life.

Piscean siblings are your kind of people. You probably have great influence over a younger sister or brother, while you appreciate an older sibling's spirituality and sense of perception.

If you want to find out more about compatibility within your family, check out the chart opposite . . .

Are you compatible with your family? Check out this destiny chart and find out . . .

Your Sign	Your perfect mum is . . .	Your perfect dad is . . .	Mum from hell is . . .	Dad from hell is . . .	Best brother is . . .	Best sister is . . .
SCORPIO	Scorpio or Pisces	Taurus or Capricorn	Cancer	Gemini	Capricorn	Sagittarius
SAGITTARIUS	Gemini or Aquarius	Aries or Leo	Taurus	Scorpio	Aquarius	Capricorn
CAPRICORN	Taurus or Capricorn	Virgo or Scorpio	Aquarius	Libra	Pisces	Aquarius
AQUARIUS	Gemini or Leo	Libra or Scorpio	Capricorn	Virgo	Aries	Pisces
PISCES	Libra or Scorpio	Pisces or Cancer	Leo	Aries	Taurus	Aries
ARIES	Aries or Leo	Libra or Sagittarius	Virgo	Pisces	Gemini	Taurus
TAURUS	Taurus or Virgo	Scorpio or Capricorn	Gemini	Sagittarius	Cancer	Gemini
GEMINI	Aries or Sagittarius	Gemini or Aquarius	Pisces	Taurus	Leo	Cancer
CANCER	Cancer or Libra	Pisces or Taurus	Sagittarius	Aquarius	Virgo	Leo
LEO	Aries or Cancer	Scorpio or Aquarius	Libra	Capricorn	Libra	Virgo
VIRGO	Cancer or Virgo	Capricorn or Taurus	Aries	Leo	Scorpio	Libra
LIBRA	Gemini or Libra	Aries or Aquarius	Scorpio	Cancer	Sagittarius	Scorpio

Your Future Family

How many times you marry, the number of children you have and whether or not you'll have a happy family in the future all depends on your Sun Sign (Scorpio) combined with your Rising Sign. Check out your Rising Sign (see pages 6–19), then check what it reveals below.

You're Scorpio with . . .

Aries Rising. Love and relationships will be extremely important to you. You give of yourself freely when you're in love. Sounds good, but this may lead to problems because you tend to be impetuous. You'll marry in a bit of a hurry while you're still young and this could lead to divorce. One or two children are forecast.

Taurus Rising. Affectionate, faithful and loyal – that's you. You'll meet your life partner early and will probably be together for a very long time. Mr Right won't be very sociable but you won't mind. Your children will be artistic.

Gemini Rising. You're such a flirt, the guys in your life will find it difficult to know when to take you seriously.

Two or three life partnerships look likely, with one liaison abroad. Your two kids will be lucky.

Cancer Rising. You're complex, emotional and feel very deeply – no wonder your relationships are complicated! You're likely to have at least two marriages or life partnerships. Children? You'll have more than two and they'll bring you great happiness.

Leo Rising. You have an enormous lust for life and tend to abandon yourself heart, body and soul. It's likely there'll be two marriages or life partnerships, with kids from each relationship. If you end up with an Aquarius, twins are a possibility.

Virgo Rising. You don't find it easy to put your feelings into words. Therefore you'll look for a partner who's sensitive and understanding. You'll find him – twice. You won't have a big family.

Libra Rising. Love is something you can't live without. That's great but the trouble is, you'll find it hard to control your wandering eye, even when you settle down. However, only one lot of wedding bells are ringing for you. Kids? One or two.

Scorpio Rising. You're romantic, passionate and sensual but you'll only show these qualities to a special few. The thing is, you love so intensely that jealousy's a problem Two marriages seem likely, with many children. Good job you like kids!

Sagittarius Rising. You'll be best off pairing off with straightforward, forthright men, but you can't resist the glamour of someone a bit more mysterious! Therefore you could have a secret affair or two as well as a couple of marriages. You won't have more than a couple of kids.

Capricorn Rising. Love intrigues you. It's something you take seriously but you find it hard to relax in the company of the opposite sex. However, when you meet your soulmate, it's likely you'll be with him for life. As you're very ambitious and career-minded, you may decide not to have children.

Aquarius Rising. Some may regard you as cold because you're not very demonstrative. You're more expressive once you've given your heart and it's likely your marriage will be happy. You enjoy travelling with your husband/partner and two kids (twins quite possibly).

Pisces Rising. Phew! You have enough love for everyone and you need a mate who'll understand you and return your passion and love. However, marriage may not be easy for you and two long-term relationships look likely. You'll have a large family who'll bring you great joy.

Pet Power!

And finally . . . pets. They're members of the family too, you know! Check the chart below and discover which animals are for you and which pets you prefer.

Your Sign	Favourite farm animal	Favourite wild animal	Perfect pet	You like a pet to be . . .
Scorpio	Goose	Shark	Tarantula or snake	Scary!
Sagittarius	Horse	Zebra	Pony or horse	Sporty
Capricorn	Goat	Crocodile	Cat	Self-sufficient
Aquarius	Donkey	Kangaroo	Tree frog	Interesting
Pisces	Sheep	Whale	Goldfish	Dependent
Aries	Ram	Rhino	Rat or mouse	Fast-moving
Taurus	Bull	Elephant	Dog	Reliable
Gemini	Collie dog	Tiger	Parrot	Responsive
Cancer	Pig	Dolphin	Rabbit	Lovable
Leo	Cockerel	Lion	Puppy	Fun
Virgo	Cow	Orang-utan	Budgie	Clean
Libra	Baby chick	Monkey	Cockatoo or dove	Pretty

Part 6:

School, Career, Hobbies, Money

Are You The Perfect Pupil?

At school, you're not happy unless you're the best at everything. You're the top of the class, the captain of the sports team, the leader of the debating society and the organizer of the end-of-term party. Certain (usually jealous) classmates think you're a right swot, but you don't care: as far as you're concerned, you're not at school to be popular.

You may not be crazy about school, but you know it's important that you attend as often as possible (you're one of the least likely signs of the zodiac to skive) and make the most of it. You're very intelligent, so you have an obvious advantage over your less bright classmates. You are determined to get on in class and take all your schoolwork very seriously. You have a natural preference for History, but tend to be pretty hot at most subjects.

You're extremely critical of your teachers, believing that most of them are pretty stupid. You don't always agree with their methods of teaching and are quite happy to say so. If you see a teacher as weak or not as clever as you (and, sadly, many of them aren't), you won't pay too much attention to them, preferring instead to swot up when you get home. In your eyes, most teacher types are viewed as a waste of space until they prove themselves otherwise . . .

You're quick to learn, naturally curious and have a great memory. This bodes well for lessons and exam-taking. In fact, as a Scorpio, you're likely to pass pretty much every exam you take, more often than not with flying colours!

If you want to see how your mates compare as schoolmates and pupils, refer to the chart opposite . . .

Just The Job

With regards to work, you're determined and aggressive, never doing anything by half and wanting success above all else.

Any job you take on needs to be absorbing, with plenty of scope for promotion and advancement. You like being with other people and wouldn't be too happy working alone. You must watch out that employers don't take advantage of your energetic personality – before you know it, you'll be doing loads of overtime for no extra pay!

You make a great leader and are often found in

Study this specially devised chart and work out what kind of student you are . . .

Your Sign	As a student you're . . .	Your fave subject is . . .	Most compatible teacher is . . .	You'd get detention for . . .	Your perfect classmate is . . .
SCORPIO	Serious and ambitious	History	A Capricornian	Being sarcastic	A Taurean
SAGITTARIUS	Nothing but trouble	Geography	An Aquarian	Not doing your homework	A Geminian
CAPRICORN	Teacher's pet!	Maths	A Piscean	Letting your work be copied	A Cancerian
AQUARIUS	A bit hard to handle	Social studies	An Arien	Skiving	A Leo
PISCES	Lazy but imaginative	Art	A Taurean	Not paying attention	A Virgoan
ARIES	Noisy but bright	PE	A Geminian	Shouting	A Libran
TAURUS	Slow but determined	Science	A Cancerian	Sulking	A Scorpian
GEMINI	Irritatingly clever	Languages	A Leo	Writing notes	A Sagittarian
CANCER	Quiet and studious	Cookery	A Virgoan	Eating sweets in class	A Capricornian
LEO	Attention-seeking	English language	A Libran	Messing about	An Aquarian
VIRGO	Chatty and hardworking	English literature	A Scorpian	Being cheeky	A Piscean
LIBRA	Lively and creative	Needlework	A Sagittarian	Rule-breaking	An Arien

charge of a team or department. If there are ever any crises to be dealt with, you're able to sort everything out in a calm and capable way. You're pretty critical of the people you work with, especially those who aren't as efficient as you, but if your own work isn't up to scratch, you'll be the first to point it out. You're a real fighter and will only give up on a job or project if you know 100 per cent that there's no hope of success. You're very ambitious and hope to get to the top of your chosen career one day.

As a boss, you expect a lot of loyalty from your employees. You're very sympathetic to any problems your workers might have and are happy to help in any way you can. You can't abide time-wasters though and will sack someone without hesitation if you believe they're not pulling their weight. It's likely you'll have a high-powered career. Suitable ones include police work, pathology, science, surgery, medicine, sport or TV research.

Hobbies

You're a busy bee and like to be occupied at all times. Not one for vegging out in front of the TV, you'd much rather be doing something constructive. You like discovering how things work, but it's not just machines that interest you:

you're also totally fascinated by the workings of the human mind. All Scorpios love reading – you can't get enough of thrillers, detective novels, and anything to do with human psychology.

Will You Be Rich?

How likely you are to get rich can depend on your star sign.

As a Scorpio, you're pretty interested in money and how to make lots of it, mainly because you want a good quality of life. You're not one of the zodiac's biggest spenders and actually prefer earning the stuff to using it.

You can be quite secretive about any dosh you make and although this can sometimes cause problems, especially in close relationships, that's just the way you are. (In fact, you're pretty secretive about most things.)

Astro-cash facts:

- The people most likely to get rich are (in this order) Leos, Taureans, Sagittarians and Virgoans. These signs are closely followed by Aries, Capricorn, Cancer, Scorpio, Libra, Gemini and Aquarius. The least likely sign to accumulate great wealth is Pisces (unless you're Cindy Crawford or Drew Barrymore, that is – both Pisceans and both rather loaded).

- Leos get richest the quickest. But they need to focus on making money and not be distracted by all the other stuff that life hurls their way.
- Cancerians are destined to get rich through their own efforts and shrewdness. They won't get rich, however, if they sit back and relax every time they have a minor success: they must keep on keeping on if they want to make it Branson-style.
- If you were born when Jupiter was in Taurus, great wealth will be yours. Jupiter was in Taurus from 12 April 1964 until 22 April 1965. It moved through the sign again from 26 March 1976 to 22 August 1976 and, again, from 17 October 1976 to 3 April 1977. It returned to Taurus on 9 March 1988 until 21 July 1988, and again from 1 December 1988 until 10 March 1989. Its most recent visit to the sign was on 28 June 1999 where it stayed until 22 October 1999. The next time this transit occurs will be from 15 February 2000 until 29 June 2000. Anyone born during any of these periods is born to be rich!

Part 7:

Holidays

Sun, Sand And Stars!

Scorpians are often reluctant to go away, but usually have a good time once they reach their holiday destination. If you want to find out which countries are a-calling, how to get there and who your top travelling companion should be, you've come to the right place . . .

You're not a born traveller or holidaymaker, and it often takes friends or family to persuade you to leave the comfort of your home for a break, but once away you really do appreciate it. Ideally, you prefer to be alone but, as this isn't always practical, many of your holidays are sort of "like it or lump it" situations. You love anything luxurious and exotic, and wouldn't be content camping or caravanning. You're able to withstand high and low temperatures, so weather doesn't really bother you too much.

Do What? (And Where?)

Somewhere you can explore is ideal for you. You love mystery and enjoy outings which enable you to make discoveries. Holidays which involve visiting anywhere that's haunted or famous palaces, museums and temples would appeal to your inquisitive nature. You love checking out caves, too, but if you don't get to see any this summer, you should search out other dark, dank, spooky places . . .

How To Get There

Because you're a Water Sign, water travel attracts you – so going abroad by ferry would appeal – but you don't mind travelling by plane, car, bus or coach. Once at your chosen destination, you like to explore in style and won't think twice about setting money aside for taxi fares.

Holiday Horrors

Scorpio folk tend to dehydrate quicker than most so, if you're somewhere hot, try to remember to drink lots of mineral water. Sunburn, too, can be a problem as you can sit in the sun for hours without feeling uncomfortable. And because you're so self-absorbed, you may exclude others – even when they're with you sometimes! Try to be less secretive about your plans and if you're travelling with someone else, try talking to them occasionally!

Best Holidays . . .

will be had in Norway, Poland and Switzerland.

Your Sign	What you need	Holiday love with . . .	Activities	Travel . . .	Holiday horrors
SCORPIO	Mystery and excitement	a Taurean	Drawing and touring	Taxi!	Dehydration (in hot countries)
SAGITTARIUS	Thrills!	a Geminian	Riding and skateboarding	by motorbike	Being conned
CAPRICORN	Peace and quiet	a Cancerian	Camping	on foot	Getting bored
AQUARIUS	Freedom	a Leo	Safari and nature treks	any way	Running out of money
PISCES	Peace and quiet	a Virgoan	Fishing and picnicking	by boat	Being disappointed
ARIES	Lots of action	a Libran	Pony-trekking and swimming	fast!	Accidents
TAURUS	Time	a Scorpian	Relaxing	slowly	Being too lazy and missing out
GEMINI	Stimulation	a Sagittarian	Socializing and sightseeing	by plane	Stomach upsets
CANCER	Homely surroundings	a Capricornian	All types of watersports	by water	Stress
LEO	Sunshine	an Aquarian	Sunbathing	in style!	Sunburn!
VIRGO	Culture	a Piscean	Skiing and snowboarding	by train	Catching lurgies
LIBRA	New experiences	an Arien	Walking and cycling	first-class	Over-indulgence, in snogging especially!

Part 8:

Party On!

Scorpio – The Serious Socializer

What's your social style? Are you a party animal or a bit of a party pooper? Read on to find out whether you (and your mates) are the life 'n' soul . . .

You often come across as cool and antisocial, but behind that steely façade lies a soft-hearted, generous and sociable individual. You may not have a million mates but the ones you do have mean the world to you. Your social circle may be small but – hey – it's the quality of your mates, not the quantity, that counts. When it comes to partying, you like to do the arranging and don't like anyone else interfering. (When it comes to needing to be in control, even bossy Leos fall behind Scorpios!) Seemingly serious, you may surprise folk when you show them how willing you are to let it all hang

out. You're a good host – in fact, you much prefer people coming to you than going out. But whatever you do and wherever you go, you'll always have a good time.

Your perfect party: An evening at your place. Food may not be a feature, but your guests won't be hungering for fun and games, that's for sure!

Craziest party stunt: Letting out a bottom burp during a game of Twister!! (oops!)

Going out . . . can be fun – but only if you've organized everything.

Staying in . . . means it's time to get to grips with a good book.

Your Partying Friends

And what about your mates? Here's a quick run-down of the other eleven signs . . .

Sagittarius

Sagittarians were made for partying. If there's a party on, they don't care where it is – they're there! They have a big reputation for getting even the sleepiest of parties going and are always in hot demand as guests.

Perfect party: Any party – anywhere!

Craziest party stunt: Travelling 500 miles to a party that wasn't actually on. (Oh dear.)

Going out . . . is their reason for living.

Staying in . . . is totally soul-destroying.

Capricorn

Partying is way down a Capricorn's list of priorities. If they *do* go out, they like to decide exactly where they're going, who they're seeing and what they're doing. Someone else's party may be full of too many surprises.

Perfect party: Home alone with a box of popcorn, a pile of magazines and the phone.

Craziest party stunt: Forgetting to bolt the toilet door.

Going out . . . is OK on special occasions.

Staying in . . . is OK any time.

Aquarius

Although they're very sociable, Aquarians aren't really that bothered about partying. They turn down more party invitations than any other sign because, in their view, they've usually got something more interesting to do.

Perfect party: A Green one. (We're talking politics here.)

Craziest party stunt: Riding down the stairs on a trike!

Going out . . . should have a purpose.

Staying in . . . is something they should do more of.

Pisces

Pisceans are laugh-a-minute party people and can bop till they drop! The Piscean attitude to socializing is forever changing though: sometimes they're positively agoraphobic; other times, they just *have* to go out.

Perfect party: At a club with a few close friends.

Craziest party stunt: Being wheeled home in a shopping trolley!

Going out . . . with a Piscean can be dangerous!

Staying in . . . is something they really need to do on occasion.

Aries

Ariens are the absolute life and soul, and the most wanted guests in town! They have the ability to turn a cosy gathering into a crazy party – they customize the atmosphere to suit themselves. And they couldn't care less what anyone thinks.

Perfect party: An all-night do in a massive club full of thousands of ravers – all close mates, of course!

Craziest party stunt: Performing their own version of

Saturday Night Fever with a mate – in their undies!

Going out . . . is what weekends are for!

Staying in . . . makes them want to go out!

Taurus

Taureans love going out, but they like plenty of warning. Preparing physically, mentally and spiritually for a big night out takes more than a few minutes for a slow-moving Taurean.

Perfect party: A karaoke do in a nice restaurant (Taureans love a good croon), then home to bed – not too late though (Taureans love a good kip too!)

Craziest party stunt: Falling asleep under the pile of coats in the spare room.

Going out . . . is a chore if they're not in the right mood; fine if they are.

Staying in . . . suits their couch-potato personality!

Gemini

All Geminians love their social lives to be varied and thrilling and if they're not, they'll get bored and grumpy. Not that they're asking to be entertained – Gems are more than happy to organize their own activities.

Perfect party: A top house party at a mate's house, where they can arrive early, get ready, and help with the proceedings.

Craziest party stunt: Copping off with every member of the opposite sex there – regardless of who they're going out with! (Tut tut!)

Going out . . . perks 'em up.

Staying in . . . gets 'em down.

Cancer

It has to be said that Cancerians aren't exactly famous for their round-the-clock partying. At the risk of appearing boring, they prefer staying in – especially if there's any eating of delicious snacks to be done!

Perfect party: A dinner party – food cooked by the Cancerian – for a few close chums.

Craziest party stunt: Staying out past midnight.

Going out . . . is unavoidable sometimes.

Staying in . . . means lots of lovely quality time . . . with themselves. Luxury!

Leo

Everyone knows how gorgeous and fun-loving Leos can be, but may *not* know what control freaks they are. Being someone else's guest can be unnerving for a Leo. On the other hand, they make totally fab hosts.

Perfect party: A party at home, with scrummy grub, plenty of dancing and Leo, as ever, in the spotlight.

Craziest party stunt: Going to someone else's party and actually enjoying it!

Going out . . . is fine if they know what to expect and can spend at least *most* of the evening being the centre of attention.

Staying in . . . is a reasonably enjoyable necessity.

Virgo

Virgos aren't 100 per cent comfortable at a rowdy party. In a Virgoan's view, parties aren't so much social occasions, but are more a way of networking. Most Virgoans prefer spending time in their own company.

Perfect party: A sleep-over with a couple of their closest girl friends.

Craziest party stunt: Dancing.

Going out . . . gives others the pleasure of their marvellous company.

Staying in . . . is boring at worst, blissful at best.

Libra

Librans are the most popular signs of the zodiac and, along with Ariens, are Numero Uno party people! Even when they don't really want to go out, it doesn't take much to persuade them.

Perfect party: Librans aren't keen on noise, so a quiet party at a hired room in a restaurant with twenty to thirty friends, some nice music and scrumptious scoff would do just fine.

Craziest party stunt: Dancing on the table, clad in nowt but a feather boa!

Going out . . . is fun but can be tiring.

Staying in . . . is great in the right company.

Part 9:

Moon Magic

Moon Rhythms

The moon is the most feminine of the planets, and its waxing and waning affects every female on earth. Check our special chart opposite and discover how it influences you. Then use some moon magic to brighten up your life . . .

Did you know that the human body is approximately 50 per cent water? And that in the same way that the waxing and waning moon pulls the tides of the sea, it can also have a serious pull on our bodies and minds. As the female of the species, we're even more fluid, what with periods and our ability to retain water. Because of this, our health and emotions are closely connected to the phases of the moon. Check the chart opposite and see when the moon's doing what from now till the end of the year 2000 . . .

The Waning Phase

During the **waning phase** (the period between a Full and a New Moon), you'll be at your most serious and probably your quietest. Time should be spent in a meditative way. Many people – females in particular – feel a bit grumpy around this time and are more prone to sulking than usual. You may find it hard to relax, even though that's exactly what you *should* be doing. Quite often, you'll find that you're very forgetful around this time. If this phase coincides with your pre-

	WANING	NEW MOON	WAXING	FULL MOON
1999				
Sep/Oct	26th–8th	9th	10th–23rd	24th
Oct/Nov	25th–7th	8th	9th–22nd	23rd
Nov/Dec	24th–6th	7th	8th–21st	22nd
Dec/Jan	23rd–5th	6th	7th–20th	21st
2000				
Jan/Feb	22nd–4th	5th	6th–18th	19th
Feb/Mar	20th–5th	6th	7th–19th	20th
Mar/Apr	21st–3rd	4th	5th–17th	18th
Apr/May	19th–3rd	4th	5th–17th	18th
May/Jun	19th–1st	2nd	3rd–15th	16th
Jun/Jul	17th–30th	1st	2nd–15th	16th
Jul/Aug	17th–30th	31st	1st–14th	15th
Aug/Sep	16th–28th	29th	30th–12th	13th
Sep/Oct	14th–26th	27th	28th–12th	13th
Oct/Nov	14th–26th	27th	28th–10th	11th
Nov/Dec	12th–24th	25th	26th–10th	11th
Dec	12th–24th	25th		

period days, everyone had best keep out of your way – you're a total ogre!

When the moon's in its waning phase . . .

. . . spend more time with your family and less with your friends

. . . rely less on others and more on your own intuition and instincts

. . . operations carried out will be very successful
. . . you're less likely to put on weight (chow down that choc!)
. . . household chores are less of a chore!

What to do

- If you're feeling stressed, do something about it.
- Avoid negative thinking and try to develop a more positive attitude.
- Give yourself some time alone. Take a long bath, listen to some soothing music or have a bit of a cry.
- If you really don't want to be alone, make a date with someone you love and have a good cuddle!

The New Moon

On the day of the **New Moon** (when the moon occupies the same sign as the Sun), you may have new beginnings on your mind. You feel extra energetic and may feel more driven or competitive than usual.

At the time of the New Moon . . .

. . . you're more chatty than usual
. . . your concentration levels are up
. . . people – girls mainly – are in a more optimistic mood
. . . you're keen to get on (procrastinators and slowcoaches will really bug you!)
. . . animals and plants thrive particularly well
. . . your body is especially strong and more resistant than usual to illness

. . . you'll have more success if you make an effort to give up any bad habits you might have

. . . you're more likely to succeed at anything you attempt

What to do

- Don't waste time – there's loads to do, so get on with it!
- Spend time with your girl friends and chat about your needs and desires. (Remember – they'll be affected by the New Moon in much the same way as you are. And you'll have a real psychic connection with mates who share your star sign.)
- Get up early, go for walks, catch up on your letter writing and make phone calls (especially the ones you've been putting off).
- Do some gardening!
- Take up a new hobby or pastime.
- Move house.
- Have another go at something you've previously failed to master. (You're sure to get the hang of it this time.)
- Grab all opportunities.
- Make up with a mate.
- Tune in to your psychic powers!
- Fall in love!

The Waxing Phase

The **waxing**, or first phase, of the moon (the period when the moon appears to grow from what looks like a little piece of toenail clipping to a big round dinner plate) is generally a very positive time.

When the moon's in its waxing phase . . .

. . . healing of wounds is slower than usual

. . . you're more likely to put on weight if you're careless about what you eat

. . . water retention and PMT are more likely to occur

. . . reactions to toxins are more dramatic

What to do

- Make big decisions.
- Make plans and set yourself goals. This may not be easy but any serious efforts made during these two weeks will almost definitely pay off.

The Full Moon

When the Sun and Moon are in opposite signs of the zodiac and the moon is as round as it can possibly be, it's said to be a **Full Moon**. At this time of the month, regardless of your own personal cycle, you're likely to be more energetic than usual. If you need to tie up any loose ends, do it while the moon is on full beam. In astrology, the Full Moon often indicates the end of a chapter of your life. It can be a sad time, but it's also a time when the old makes way for the new. The Full Moon often indicates that some fab new experiences are coming your way. You should be at your most confident and self-assured and determined enough to succeed in whatever way you want to succeed.

At the time of the Full Moon . . .

. . . you're more likely to sleepwalk

. . . if you cut yourself, you'll bleed more than usual

. . . your period (if you're having one at the time) will be heavier

. . . you're more likely to give birth (if you're pregnant, that is)

What to do

- Surround yourself with bright colours and with people you love.
- Involve yourself in activities that are fun but don't cost too much.
- The Full Moon is a great time for partying! So party!
- Sort out your money problems.
- Expect good news.
- Make some changes at home.
- End that so-called romance (especially if you don't even like the bloke that much).
- Face up to the truth.

Moon Superstitions And Omens

- Never plant anything during the moon's waning phase – it won't grow to its full potential.
- The best time to get a haircut is on the day of the New Moon. Book that appointment now!
- The best marriages start just after a Full Moon.
- A baby born at the Full Moon will grow up to be very

strong. It's also said that if a moon is shining at the time of birth, the baby will be a boy; if there's no moon it'll be a girl. (Never mind genetics, eh?)

- If you steal anything on the third day after a New Moon, you'll most definitely be caught.
- To dream of the Full Moon foretells happiness in love; to dream of the waxing moon means a change for the better; dreaming of the waning moon indicates a change for the worse.
- It's reckoned that the moon can be used to forecast the weather. For example, if the moon is surrounded by a single misty ring, rain's on its way; several circles around the moon predict wet and stormy weather; if the New Moon falls on a Monday (as it did in November 1996 and April and September 1997), it signifies good news and good weather; and if the moon is bright yellow in a cloudless sky, good weather is imminent. Who needs Michael Fish when you've got the Man in the Moon?!
- There are many stories about who the "man in the moon" actually is. The Chinese say he's an old man who binds married couples with silken cord; the Masai of Kenya say he's not a man at all, but a woman with swollen lips and a missing eye – injuries inflicted upon her by her husband, the Sun; and some Germans believe he's an old man who has offended God and is eternally imprisoned on the moon. Quite.
- Turning silver over at the time of a New Moon encourages money to come your way. So check your chart and get flipping!

Part 10:

Your Year Ahead: The Year 2000 At A Glance

Jan 1
2000

The coming twelve months are an action-packed time for Scorpians. *With eclipses in January and July; Jupiter changing signs in February and June; and Saturn making transits in August and October, you can expect major happenings galore! For each month of the year, you get a monthly feature, an in-depth week-by-week analysis, as well as an at-a-glance weekly chart to make planning ahead easier. Have a happy year!*

JANUARY 2000

New Year, New You!

Stuck for New Year resolution ideas? Then get a load of these . . .

As a **Scorpian**, you can be incredibly suspicious of everyone and everything. That's why, as the New Year dawns, you should make an effort to be more trusting. You're so paranoid, you think everyone's out to get you. But there are plenty of folk out there who have no intention of tripping you up at all. Your New Year's resolution? To start believing that a lot of people really *do* have faith in you.

Sagittarians have enormous big mouths, which they are forever putting their huge size 12s in! The Saggie resolution for the coming year should be to be less "honest" – and to get their feet surgically trimmed. (Only joking . . . about the feet, that is!)

Capricornians secretly love putting a damper on other people's high spirits. They also love saying "no" for the sake of it. Their New Year's resolution for the year 2000 must be to say "yes, please" instead of "oooh, not for me thanks – I'm trying to give up" once in a while.

Aquarians like being cool, but sometimes they go below freezing point. They should try being more cuddly and affectionate this year.

Pisceans never know when to stop. In the year 2000, all Pisceans, should make "I think I've gone far enough now, thanks" their own personal slogan. (And get a T-shirt printed if necessary.)

Ariens are impatient little tykes and should stop drumming their fingers on table tops and hopping from foot to foot in bus queues and try to chill out a bit this year.

Taureans are clumsy, stubborn and lazy. So if they want to make some improvements, the question is: where do they start? Any resolution will do really . . .

Geminians are always flitting around, calling people they don't like in the slightest "daaarling" and kissing the air. So, really, their New Year's resolution should be to stop being so superficial. NOW!

Cancerians never stop droning on about their terrible lot in life. So the best New Year resolution for a moany old crab? To stop blubbing over nothing and being such an old drama queen!

Leos are too bossy for their own pants. If they're going to make a New Year resolution, they should remember not to treat other people like servants. (Unless they ask very nicely, of course . . .)

Virgoans love pick, pick, picking holes. If they're not careful, everything around them will soon look rather

Key to Symbols

LOVE:

Snog overload

Kiss him with caution

Not a lotta totty

FRIENDS:

Little Miss Popular

All's fine and dandy

Watch what you say

SOCIAL LIFE:

Prepare to partee!

Stay cool – don't overdo it

Time to stay in 'n' chill

colander-like. Their New Year resolution should be to at least *try* saying nice things to people occasionally.

Librans are lazy lunks and should resolve to get up out of the midden they live in and have a darn good spring-clean. And they should have a bath while they're at it!

JANUARY FORECAST

1st–7th

Mars changes signs on the 4th of January and you're hot, hot, hot! Love is coming your way by the bucket-load and you can't get enough of the opposite sex. If you want someone, go get 'em! They're putty in your hands. (Oh, and make it your New Year's resolution to start the year as you mean to go on . . .)

Love:  ***Friends:***  ***Social life:*** 

8th–14th

This week Saturn, the planet of responsibility, changes direction in the love part of your chart, and advises you to go carefully if you want to make a good impression on the guy you love. If you've had a minor row with him, kiss and make up before it's too late.

Love: 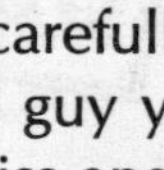 ***Friends:*** 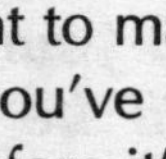 ***Social life:*** 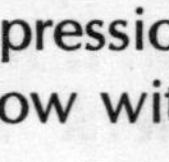

15th–21st

Mercury in the domestic part of your chart makes this week a good one to make amends with any relatives you've been having trouble with. You're at your most

See page 176 for key to symbols

persuasive and eloquent, so use your "talents" not only to get your own way but to charm your way back into their hearts . . .

Love:  ***Friends:***  ***Social life:*** 

22nd–31st

The Sun and Mercury in the home and family section of your chart mean all problems are finally resolved with close relatives (namely parents and/or siblings). In fact, being with your family is your top pastime. (Which is lucky, because right now you may not have much choice *but* to be with them.)

Love:  ***Friends:***  ***Social life:*** 

FEBRUARY 2000

Funny Valentines

Did you know that your star sign determines the sort of Valentine you'd make? Look up your sign and check whether you'll be giving or receiving (or both) this February 14th.

As an intense **Scorpian**, you just love all the mystery, intrigue and question marks that surround Valentine's Day. You don't have a huge, overriding need to be appreciated and actually get a bit embarrassed when people get all grateful. So anyone who receives a card from you will never, ever know who it's from . . .

See page 176 for key to symbols

Sagittarians don't expect to get any cards and only send them if they're under immense pressure. They're notoriously lazy and unreliable too. If someone paid them a lot of money, maybe they'd send one. But then again, maybe they still wouldn't bother.

Capricornians will always send V. Day gifts (on the right day too!), but they don't like to buy anything too expensive, too tacky or too imaginative. Looks like a nice box of chocs is the order of the day then . . .

Aquarians like to throw Valentine's Day parties, then pretend they forgot it was Valentine's Day, then get loads of cards and love gifts from all their guests and not give out any themselves. Very clever . . .

Pisceans are real old sops: they not only pen the verses in the cards they send, but they also make the cards themselves out of a pair of their old frilly pants. Then they write a song, record it on a cassette, sellotape it inside the card and send the whole shiboodle to their "cherie amour". (Pass the sick bucket please . . .)

Ariens are sexy but not particularly romantic. They prefer saucy underwear to a 'ickle teddy bear with "I Wuv Oo" embroidered on its furry tum. If they actually *remember* V. Day, they'll probably forget the card, flowers and chocs and buy their loved one something small and frothy instead (and we're not talking milkshakes here).

Taureans are extremely romantic and very sensual. Not only will they be buying their Valentine flowers and jewels, but they'll probably stretch to a jar of chocolate body paint too. Mmmm . . . delish!

Geminians think V. Day is v. exciting, but only if they get tons of cards from secret admirers. The thing is though – they're so busy thinking about themselves, they clean forget to buy anything for their paramours. (Oops!)

Cancerians are extremely romantic and will be arranging all sorts of lovely slushy surprises for their darling. A candlelit dinner, a stroll in the moonlight and snogs a-plenty – that's what they'll be giving their sweetheart on V. Day.

Leos are madly extravagant and love to splash out on their loved ones. The trouble is that they do need a bit of a nudge sometimes. If a lovestruck someone dropped them a line (or a hint) prior to the big day, they'd be only too happy to oblige with love gifts a-plenty. Otherwise, they might not bother . . .

Virgoans are a bit stingy, so if the person they love is waiting by their letterbox for flowers, choccies and heart-shaped cushions with balloons attached with loads of love from a Virgoan paramour, they could be waiting a very long time indeed!

Librans are just about the silliest, slushiest, most romantic sign of the zodiac. If a lissome and lovely Libran was to be your Valentine, they'd go the whole hog, don a frilly apron and be your love slave for the day, whether that's what you wanted or not . . .

FEBRUARY FORECAST

1st–7th

Mercury joins Mars in your astrological house of health and advises you to really look after yourself. Many Scorpians are destined to suffer headaches under this transit. So take it easy if you can.

Love:  ***Friends:***  ***Social life:*** 

8th–14th

This week's Full Moon suggests it's high time you took a close look at some of your so-called "mates'. Some of them haven't really got your interests at heart and are only hanging out with you for selfish reasons. One friendship may have to end, but this just leaves a gap which will soon be filled by someone new – and less selfish. The effect of the total eclipse in the social part of your chart tells you that it's time to make some major changes to your social life. News you receive before the end of the week confirms this. Mars changes signs and your attitude towards health and lifestyle changes too. Maybe you're thinking about turning veggie or spending more time exercising.

Love:  ***Friends:***  ***Social life:*** 

15th–21st

Jupiter enters your opposite sign and sees you entering an important – not to mention romantic – phase of your life. Stay optimistic and things will go from good to

See page 176 for key to symbols

better. Venus in the domestic part of your chart bodes well for all family get-togethers. If a relative is celebrating this week, you'll have fun celebrating with them. Anything to do with weddings or engagements is especially well-starred.

Love:  ***Friends:***  ***Social life:*** 

22nd–29th

It's a very quiet time for you and that's probably for the best. So much has been going on in your life lately, you could do with a rest. So take one while you can . . .

Love:  ***Friends:***  ***Social life:*** 

MARCH 2000

Don't Forget Mother's Day!

March is for mums – so don't forget to buy her something gorgeous on M. Day itself. If you're stuck for ideas, consider these . . .

Arien mums aren't as frumpy as they sometimes look and would be quite distressed if you bought them a nice oven glove or apron for Mother's Day. Buy them the latest Verve CD though and they'd be well flattered.

Taurean mums are very practical and like gardening, so a nice trowel would be the ideal Mother's Day gift.

See page 176 for key to symbols

They're also partial to a bit of chocolate, so a *chocolate* trowel would be even better.

Geminian mums like surprises and would hate anything as clichéd as flowers or chocolates. They love a good read – nothing too heavy, mind – and would really appreciate an annual subscription to a posh magazine.

Cancerian mums are real home lovers, so anything for the house would be a good gift. Food goes down a treat – especially the gourmet variety – as does a nice leafy plant. Easy to please or what?

Leo mums aren't too bothered about what pressie you actually buy them: as long as it's BIG, they'll be totally impressed by it. They also like anything glittery, shiny or sparkly – never mind the quality, it's the size and the UV factor that matters.

Virgoan mums just *love* tidying up. They like their bodies, homes and cars to be sweet-smelling and clean at all times. If your ma's a Virgo, buy her a nice bar of soap, a mini-vac or a Magic Tree air freshener for the car.

Libran mums adore being fussed over and love receiving cards (home-made ones are their faves). On Mother's Day, tell her she looks gorgeous and that you love her, then present her with your latest artistic masterpiece. She'll be completely chuffed.

Scorpian mums like curling up on the sofa with a good book. For Mother's Day, find out her favourite author and buy her a copy of his/her most recent novel. (Make sure she hasn't got it already though. Scorpio mums have a sneaky habit of buying books on the quiet.)

Sagittarian mums really aren't fussy about what presents they get. As far as they're concerned, it's the thought that counts. If you remember Mother's Day at all, they'll be over the moon. And if you can't stretch to a costly gift, a big kiss and a "love you, Mum" will do just fine.

Capricornian mums, it has to be said, are slightly martyrish. They'll say (well in advance of Mother's Day) "No, really, Mother's Day – pah! I don't believe in it – I'd be much happier if you didn't get me anything . . . " but then they get really upset when you do as you're told. So ignore what she says. Make a big fuss of her. Make her a cake. Buy her flowers. It'll make your life a lot easier all round.

Aquarian mums are pretty charitable types. If you told her you weren't going to buy her a Mother's Day present, but that you were going to donate some money to her favourite charity instead, she'd be well impressed. But secretly she'd be equally thrilled with a comedy video, CD or diary.

Piscean mums are dreamy and romantic, and really look forward to Mother's Day. Make it worth waiting for by presenting her with a book of romantic poetry, a bottle of champagne or a big bunch of lilies. Whatever you buy, make sure it's wrapped nicely – Pisceans love a bit of fancy wrapping.

MARCH FORECAST

11st–7th

The New Moon and the Sun in the romance part of your chart means a romance is on the cards. If you're boy-free, you could well meet someone really cute this week. If you're seeing someone, you may just fall in love. Aw . . .

Love:  ***Friends:***  ***Social life:*** 

8th–14th

As Mercury joins the Sun in your astrological house of fun and frolics, you're in the mood for love. Work is a definite no-no, so being at school is quite painful – especially if there's some unfinished business to be be dealt with . . . If there is, don't leave it any longer: deal with it now – it could be your last chance.

Love:  ***Friends:***  ***Social life:*** 

15th–21st

The Sun in the health part of your chart sees you making a recovery from a minor ailment. You're raring to go, which is a good thing, as you've a lot on your plate right now.

Love:  ***Friends:***  ***Social life:*** 

22nd–31st

Energetic Mars enters your opposite sign, causing all

See page 176 for key to symbols

sorts of arguments between you and close mates and/or boyfriend/s. It might be an idea to try to reach a compromise before the end of the month. Easter could be a painful affair otherwise . . .

Love:  ***Friends:***  ***Social life:*** 

APRIL 2000

Are You An Easter Chick?

The Easter hols are here, which means lots of choc and no school. Great! Not so great though is the constant round of visiting relatives and night after night of tedious TV. Read on to discover whether Easter is your "thing" . . .

As a **Scorpian**, you really like the fact that everything goes a bit quiet over Easter and that you can relax for a short moment in your otherwise hectic life. Trouble is, year after year, you always invite tons of relatives round for celebratory drinks and snacks, thus making Easter more hard work than any other time of year. And you never learn either . . .

Sagittarians, unless deeply religious, couldn't give a monkey's about Easter. They're more than likely to use the time off to go somewhere as far away from home as possible (somewhere they don't celebrate Easter preferably . . .)

See page 176 for key to symbols

Capricornians don't particularly like Easter but feel it's their duty to celebrate it. This means doing all the traditional stuff associated with the festival, such as baking hot cross buns, giving (and scoffing) Easter eggs, and having people round for tea. Then moaning about it. A lot.

Aquarians like having time off from school, but aren't overly bothered about celebrating Easter in the traditional way. No, they're more likely to use the hols as a time to catch up on the soaps, read a couple of books and update their diary.

Pisceans enjoy privacy, so the thought of a whole barrage of relatives coming over for Easter Sunday lunch sends shivers up their sensitive little spines. Ideally, they'd spend the hols lolling around in a negligee, daintily munching on a few Milk Tray and saying "I want to be alone".

Ariens love the holidays, but can't abide Easter itself. It's the crap telly that upsets them the most. All those variety performances! Breaking up from school is fab – there's no denying that. But it's all downhill after that really.

Taureans' favourite part of the Easter break is all the lovely chocolate! They're determined to eat as many Easter eggs as is humanly possible and then spend the rest of the hols feeling bilious. Mmm . . . fun . . .

Geminians like the excitement surrounding Easter but, unless they're religious types, can't really understand what all the fuss is about. If the Easter

Bunny was real though . . . now that'd be a different matter altogether.

Cancerians love a nice family get-together, so if there are any rellos visiting or to be visited, Cancer will be in their element. The best bit about Easter, as far as they're concerned, is all the home-made cakes (especially the hot cross buns). Yum!

Leos see Easter as an opportunity to buy their nearest and dearest some lovely choccy gifts. It's a little-known astrological fact that most people who shop at Thornton's over the Easter period are Leos. (Maybe.)

Virgoans think Easter is a silly and frivolous waste of time. In their opinion, it's a waste of valuable school time and if they had their way, there wouldn't be any Easter holidays at all. (The summer hols would be extended by two weeks instead.)

Librans like everything to do with Easter – the cards, the Easter eggs, the "Jesus" films on TV and the family gatherings. Why it's just like Christmas, but with daffodils and bunnies and little fluffy yellow chicks. (OK, that's enough, Libra!)

APRIL FORECAST

1st–7th

The New Moon in the health part of your chart has you feeling on top of the world. Ease yourself back into things slowly though: if you rush it, you could get ill again.

Love:  **Friends:**  **Social life:** 

8th–14th

Venus's transit on the 8th focuses on your health and advises you to eat well, sleep lots and take it easy on the socializing front. School's well-starred at the moment, as long as you make sure you don't give into laziness. Get set for some hard graft . . . Mercury is in your astrological house of health and this could mean another minor malady. You're a bit stressed out and should stop taking on so much. OK, so there's a lot to do, but maybe it's time to let someone else take the strain – for a few days anyway.

Love:  **Friends:**  **Social life:** 

15th–21st

Mercury and Venus in the health part of your chart all week long means you should take it easy if you want to avoid coming down with horrible lurgies. Stop taking on so much – let others take the strain sometimes. The Sun in your opposite sign bodes well for all close relationships. If you've been a bit selfish with regards to your best mate, now's the time to apologize. Boyfriend problems will be solved too, as long as you're willing to compromise – at least a little bit. Try it – it might be worth it . . .

Love:  **Friends:**  **Social life:** 

See page 176 for key to symbols

22nd–30th

With an amazing five planets – the Sun, Mercury, Mars, Jupiter and Saturn – in your opposite sign by Sunday the 30th, romance is extremely well-starred. If you're dating someone, this could be love. If you're single, you won't be for much longer. Brace yourself . . .

Love:  ***Friends:***  ***Social life:*** 

MAY 2000

Spring Fever!

At this time of the year, all the signs of the zodiac tend to get a tad frisky. Some more than others . . .

As a **Scorpio**, you're one of the zodiac's top sexpots. You're easily aroused and start to feel your sap rising at the mere *mention* of spring. Almost all of the opposite sex become irresistibly attractive to you at this time of year and many of you start a passionate romance in May. Come summer though, you often realize what a mistake you've made. (Oops!)

Sagittarians get itchy feet (and we're not talking athlete's foot here) in the spring and can't wait to get away. Many of them *have* to wait though, so at this time of year their craziness isn't due so much to spring fever, as to the fact that they can't do as they want.

Capricornians are *never* crazy: they're just too sensible to let anything – spring included – make them behave

See page 176 for key to symbols

out of character. They might – just *might* – turn up the volume on their transistor radio a smidgen, but that's about as far as it goes.

Aquarians are pretty crazy at the best of times, so the time of year doesn't really make much difference. Spring sometimes brings out their creative side though, and many an Aquarian will be seen sporting a beret and brandishing a paintbrush in May.

Pisceans would spend the whole of spring in Paris if they could – it's just *sooo* romantic there (so they've heard). If they haven't a paramour at this time of year, they'll spend every waking hour searching for one. Spring fever at its worst . . .

Ariens are seriously affected by the warmer weather and can go a bit crazy if not carefully monitored. Arien females can't get enough of the boys at this time of year and seem to fancy every single one they see. Careful now . . .

Taureans feel the effects of the spring – there's no denying that. But the only action they're likely to take is to swap their 13-tog duvet for a 10-tog one, then to snuggle back down . . .

Geminians go ever so slightly bonkers when the spring kicks in. All they want to do is go out and have a good time. (So what's new then?)

Cancerians are seriously affected by the spring, in that all they can think about is redecorating. Come May, there's a huge increase in the number of folk hanging out at B&Q, and, guess what – most of them are Cancerians. Allegedly.

Leos, at the first sign of warm weather, start stripping off and baring their bods to the sunshine. They don't actually care if the rest of the world is still wearing its anorak – a string vest and Bermuda shorts will do Leo just fine.

Virgoans go mad in the spring all right. All they want to do is spring-clean. "That spring sunshine doesn't half show up the dust", you'll hear them say at least twelve times a day, as they gad about brandishing a feather duster.

Librans find this time of year the most romantic time of all. If they don't go actively looking for love in May, then they'll hole themselves up at home with a big stack of weepy black-and-white movies and a pile of lace hankies, and get soppy on their own instead.

MAY FORECAST

1st–7th

If you've been hoping to set the record straight with a certain guy, do it now, as Mercury has entered your opposite sign, making it easier to talk to people of the opposite sex. A weekend away might be a good idea – you need to take a breather.

Love:  ***Friends:***  ***Social life:*** 

8th–14th

This week, Mercury leaves your opposite sign and

See page 176 for key to symbols

Neptune starts going retrograde through the romance part of your chart. This would suggest that although you're at your most attractive and love is within easy reach, you're having trouble connecting with the guy you fancy. If there's any pretence going on, this could be the problem. Come clean: it'll be for the best . . .

Love:  ***Friends:***  ***Social life:*** 

15th–21st

Mercury changes signs and surrounds you with secrets. Luckily, you're good at keeping schtum (which is very frustrating for close mates who are desperate for gossip – especially that Gemini friend of yours!) No matter how much you're tempted to blab, keep quiet – you'll get into big trouble otherwise. The Full Moon could mean the end of a budding romance, but sadly you knew it was a destination-nowhere thing from the start anyway, so you're hardly surprised.

Love:  ***Friends:***  ***Social life:*** 

22nd–31st

You're at your most sexy, thanks to this week's Venus transit. You're a big hit with everyone you meet – especially members of the opposite sex – and can use your sex appeal to get your own way in every situation. (Nothing new there then . . .)

Love:  ***Friends:***  ***Social life:*** 

See page 176 for key to symbols

JUNE 2000

. . . And Don't Forget Father's Day Either!

If you want to buy your Dad a special gift on Father's Day, why bother when he'd much rather you did something else? Want to know more? Then keep reading . . .

Arien dads quite like the idea of Father's Day. In fact, they like the idea of anything that means they're the focus of everyone's attention. If your Pop's an Arien, he's no exception. He's not bothered about pressies though – he'd much rather you challenged him to a game of footie down the park.

Taurean dads find all that Father's Day malarkey a bit embarrassing and would prefer it if you just let him have an extra long lie-in – all day preferably – then brought him the papers and a nice cup of tea. (Aw, he doesn't ask for much, does he?)

Geminian dads aren't usually around much, but they'd really appreciate a phone call (wherever they might be). Cheap if he's in Bognor – a tidy sum if he's in Bangladesh!

Cancerian dads love photos, so take him down to the photo booth at Woolies, get a strip of funny "instant" pics of you and him pulling funny faces, and stick 'em in a photo album. A lovely and unusual gift that costs not very much.

Leo dads like their kids to appreciate them. Usually they like really big, expensive presents, but if you could spend the whole of Father's Day telling him what a top bloke he is and how he's the best dad in the cosmiverse, you could save yourself a whole load of cash.

Virgoan dads enjoy intellectual pursuits, so on Father's Day, instead of buying him a mug with "The World's No. 1 Dad" emblazoned on it, pretend you're Magnus Magnusson and invite him to appear on your own special edition of *Mastermind.* (He'll think he's in heaven!)

Libran dads love people doing things for them. On Father's Day, ask him if there's anything he wants doing and he's sure to present you with a big, long list. After cleaning the car, polishing his shoes (all of them) and filing all his bills, you'll be fed up, but he'll have had a nice time.

Scorpian dads love winning so, on Father's Day, challenge him to a game of Scrabble or three and let him win. He'll be *sooo* happy!

Sagittarian dads love a pint. So take him down the pub and give him a couple of quid to buy himself one. (If you're under age and not allowed in, you can sit outside in the car with a bag of crisps and a bottle of pop till he's finished.)

Capricornian dads really enjoy curries. They're a bit

expensive from the local takeaway mind, so why not attempt to make your own from ingredients already in your kitchen cupboard? Look to your mum's Madhur Jaffrey cookbook for inspiration . . .

Aquarian dads really like dancing. The only problem is, they're not very good at it and usually end up looking like right plonkers! On Father's Day, allow him to dance to his heart's content – and *don't* laugh (not even a little bit).

Piscean dads' preferred pastime is watching videos. On Father's Day, hire a few of his all-time fave movies and let him watch them till his eyes go square. Then return the vids to the hire shop for him: that's the bit he hates most.

JUNE FORECAST

1st–7th

The New Moon in the passion part of your chart signifies the occurrence of a major chemistry thing with a sexy guy (and we're not talking test tubes and bunsen burners here!). If you're single, this is great news, but if you're already seeing someone, this meeting could cause complications. Bear in mind that this attraction may not last. Consider: is it worth upsetting everyone and everything for a few moments of passion?

Love:  ***Friends:***  ***Social life:*** 

See page 176 for key to symbols

8th–14th

A positive aspect between the Moon and your ruling planet Pluto mid-week means you're feeling mighty emotional. You may come to some important realizations about yourself. Many Scorpians will have some kind of psychic experience this week. So don't be alarmed if something weird happens . . .

Love: ***Friends:*** ***Social life:***

15th–21st

The Full Moon in your astrological house of money suggests that your spending is getting out of hand. OK, so you want to splash out on pressies for those you love, but you're not Madonna, y'know. Spend within your means – *make* presents if necessary: no one's going to judge you on how much the gifts you give them are worth. (And if they do, you shouldn't be giving them gifts in the first place!)

Love: ***Friends:*** ***Social life:***

22nd–30th

Venus in the travel part of your chart forecasts time away from home. Many Scorpians will be taking a holiday away from home; others will be expanding their horizons in other ways. Whatever you do, you're likely to end up a whole lot wiser for it.

Love: ***Friends:*** ***Social life:***

See page 176 for key to symbols

JULY 2000

What Sort Of Shopper Are You?

Now the summer sales are on, will you be dashing out spending? Much of your shopping style depends on your star sign. For example . . .

All **Scorpians** have a reputation for being very careful with their cash. You like to make out you're not really a big spender, preferring to save instead . . . Secretly though, you *love* to spend – saving your money, then blowing it all in a single day! Big purchases appeal to you the most – the more expensive, the better.

Sagittarians shop in a most haphazard fashion, and can spend hours running about, not knowing what they want or what to buy. They buy a lot of things that they think will come in handy, but most of the stuff they come home with is, in fact, pretty useless.

Capricornians are the most cautious shoppers of all and don't really like to part with their hard-earned dosh, preferring instead to save it all up. Purchases are made only when necessary, and the word "spree" doesn't actually feature in their vocabulary. And, although prudent, they're the most likely sign to avoid the sales.

Aquarians can be a tad antisocial and would rather do their shopping by mail order than fighting the high street crowds. Computer-literate Aquarians surf the nternet and shop that way – then get the goods delivered to their door. More civilized by far!

Pisceans are daydreamers. They tend to get an idea of what it is they want to buy, then spend most of their lives looking for it. Chances are, their dream purchase doesn't actually exist! But because they love browsing, they don't really care.

Arien shoppers are incredibly impatient. You won't be found waiting in a long queue to pay for *anything* – not even the world's best bargain. They're naturally impulsive too, which means they've got a wardrobe-full of purchases that never should have been.

Taureans like to take their time when they go on a spree, and enjoy making a day of it – starting early, stopping for a snack, then continuing to browse. When they find something they like, they splash out. Otherwise, that purse remains tightly shut.

Geminians can spend a record amount of cash in a very limited time but sometimes lose their sense of judgment in the process. They love shopping and usually return with armloads of stuff – most of which will stay in the carrier bags for ever more!

Cancerian folk are careful shoppers and won't buy unless they're sure they really *will* use their purchase. They don't mind spending a lot – as long as it's on themselves. Buying presents for others is *not* their speciality by any stretch of the imagination.

Leo shoppers are wildly extravagant – always ready to treat themselves and others – and will always spend far more than they mean to. In fact, if someone goes out for a packet of Rolos and comes back with half of Miss Selfridge, chances are they're a Leo.

Virgoans are extremely fussy and, when shopping, will to and fro between shops for hours. Unless the potential purchase is perfect in every way and has a myriad of uses, they won't buy it. Fact: Virgoans are the shoppers most likely to return home empty-handed.

Librans like shopping and can be extravagant when the mood takes them. They're real ditherers, though, and because they find it hard to make up their minds, they often buy everything in sight (just in case) and end up very confused – not to mention broke.

JULY FORECAST

1st–7th

Jupiter's transit on the 30th of June is now causing your destiny to fall into the hands of someone close to you. Wherever they go, you're sure to follow . . .

Love:  ***Friends:***  ***Social life:*** 

8th–14th

With gorgeous planet Venus getting cosy in the "power" part of your chart, everything's going your way. Make the most of your looks and charm – these qualities alone could win you big prizes. Add them to your other talents and you can't fail! It's time to make some money too, so squeeze this week for all it's worth!

Love:  ***Friends:***  ***Social life:*** 

See page 176 for key to symbols

15th–21st

This week's eclipse causes minor communication problems. Are you trying to get hold of someone and failing? Has a letter gone astray? Phone, fax or computer not working? Then blame it on the eclipse . . .

Love: ***Friends:*** ***Social life:***

22nd–31st

The Sun changes signs and makes you extra strong and determined. You may be tempted to fake it in some way (it could make your life so much easier), but the planets advise you to be yourself at all times. Any kind of pretence will soon backfire on you and ruin your plans. So be real!

Love: ***Friends:*** ***Social life:***

AUGUST 2000

Holiday Romance

To some people, the summer is all about love. Are you the sort to indulge in a holiday romance? It all depends on your star sign . . .

You **Scorpians** are sexy enough to know you can have a holiday romance if you want one, but chances are, you're just not interested. You like to have a good time when you're on holiday and having an affair just detracts from this in your opinion. You take love

See page 176 for key to symbols

seriously and won't have a fling just for the fun of it. You like to holiday alone and won't stand for being pestered by any local romeos.

Sagittarians see holiday romances as just one of their many hobbies! If they see someone they fancy on holiday (and they usually do – on the first day more often than not!), they get to work quickly. Language differences pose no problems for them – they're quite adept at interpreting body language!

Capricornians go on holiday to see the sights, sample the culture and have a good time. Having a holiday fling doesn't really come into it. They're cautious by nature and believe that brief holiday encounters are quite risky. That's why they avoid them like the plague.

Aquarians don't often holiday in very romantic places, but if they happen to come across a bloke who shares their interests and beliefs, they won't mind seeing him once or twice during the holiday. Aquarians in a relationship may need to holiday alone; it's not just school they need a break from!

Pisceans, whether attached or single, are always in demand when on holiday. They're very romantic and love the idea of a holiday romance, but the passionate affair they envisage often turns out to be no more than a rather depressing one-night (or two-week) stand. If they take a boyfriend on holiday, their "grass is always greener" attitude could cause a row or two. (Yikes!)

Ariens love an adventure of the romantic variety and

what better way to indulge than to have a holiday romance? If you go on holiday with a boyfriend, the whole thing will be a bit of a snogsome affair. If they go without a bloke, their holiday becomes one great flirtathlon!

Taureans want a good time and if a romance happens whilst on holiday, it's a bonus. They don't go out of their way to find a bloke, but they'll certainly indulge in a fair bit of flirting. If they take a boyfriend on holiday with them, they'll be all over each other; if they go away single, they're likely to come back in love.

Geminians are the biggest flirts of the zodiac. Holiday romances were made for them. The thing they like most about summer flings is their brevity and the fact that they don't have to see the bloke ever again! Few Gemini girls take a boyfriend away with them but, with or without a boyfriend in tow, Miss Gemini will have a whale of a time.

Cancerians often fantasize about meeting a handsome foreigner and falling in love and, because of that, holiday romance is a serious business for them. They're destined to have several romances abroad. They're convinced they're the "real thing" and are disappointed when they discover they're not. If they holiday with a boyfriend, they'll only have eyes for him; if they go in search of love, they'll find it in one form or another.

Leos, when they get involved with someone on

holiday, enjoy the snogging but rarely fall in love. If they go away with a boyfriend, they'll spend half their time eating, the other half snogging. If they go blokeless, they make sure they have fun – and that includes dancing the night away, attempting to pull every half-decent bloke in sight!

Virgoans don't really like foreign affairs, but that doesn't mean they completely rule out the chance of holiday romance. They're not into casual relationships or one-night stands, and as many holiday love scenarios *are* casual, Virgoans go out of their way not to get involved. Holidaying with a boyfriend is more their thing; and they'd rather stay at home than go on holiday alone.

Librans love the idea of a holiday romance. A romance abroad is a romance made in heaven as far as they're concerned. Flirtatious by nature, they love the thrill of the chase and when they go on holiday, they don't stop running for a second! They tend to get involved very quickly though, and this can lead to many regrets.

AUGUST FORECAST

1st–7th

When Mercury changes signs, your attention turns to school. You know what you're capable of, so why don't you stretch yourself and prove it? If school's a bore, talk to a teacher and see if they can offer any solutions.

Love:  ***Friends:***  ***Social life:*** 

See page 176 for key to symbols

8th–14th

With Venus in the friends part of your chart, you're in for some fun and mischief. All your worries melt away and your mates (Taurean and Libran ones in particular) are extra supportive. Saturn leaves your opposite sign on the 10th and advises you to pay attention to money matters. You could also be having problems with your boyfriend or best mate, but that's because you're too scared to tell them how you really feel. It might be hard, but it's important that you let them know where they stand. Oh, and be gentle with them . . .

Love:  ***Friends:***  ***Social life:*** 

15th–21st

Mercury in the friends part of your chart causes you to ask whether certain mates really have your interests at heart. It also makes you question whether you really have the same beliefs as your mates: if you haven't, why do you pretend you have?

Love:  ***Friends:***  ***Social life:*** 

22nd–31st

As the Sun changes signs, you're in hot demand with your mates and the boys, so the weekend is a great time to party. Meeting new people and taking on new hobbies are well-starred too. So go for it! You won't be disappointed. This week's New Moon means you don't intend to get involved with anything you might consider dull. Planning for the future excites you,

See page 176 for key to symbols

especially when you meet someone who could be a massive help to you . . .

Love:  ***Friends:***  ***Social life:*** 

SEPTEMBER 2000

Star Students

September means one thing: no more summer holidays. School – depending on your star sign – brings either great sadness or great joy. Find out how you'll be feeling as the new term begins . . .

You'd be the first to admit that **Scorpians** are swots. With your photographic memory, you were made for learning and just love remembering great long lists of dates and formulae. And as for exams – why, they're a complete doddle! (Most frequently heard refrain from Teach: "Take this certificate of merit and go to the top of the class!")

Sagittarians detest school. They're the naughtiest people in the class and can be extremely disruptive. They drive even the most tolerant teacher to distraction because they never, *ever* do as they're told. (Most frequently heard refrain from Teach: "What's your excuse *this* time?")

Capricornians are the teachers' pets of the zodiac. They're quiet and studious, yet strangely not very

See page 176 for key to symbols

bright. Despite this, all their mates copy from them. (Most frequently heard refrain from Teach: "Why has everyone else in the class got the same (wrong) answers as you?")

Aquarians like doing everything their own way and that doesn't go down too well with the teachers. They also love skiving. In fact, given the choice, they wouldn't bother with school at all. (Most frequently heard refrain from Teach: "Where were you yesterday during double biology?")

Pisceans love doodling and writing poetry. But that's about it. Ask them to do anything involving numbers, chemicals or common sense and they blow a fuse. (Most frequently heard refrain from Teach: "Recite the chemical symbol for potassium chloride and tuck those wires back in your ears!")

Ariens are excellent at PE. If "attention-seeking" was a subject, you'd be great at that too. If they didn't enjoy sitting in the back row of the class so much, they'd be grade A students. (Most frequently heard refrain from Teach: "Come and sit at the front right NOW!")

Taureans progress slowly but surely with most subjects, but if they want to excel they'll have to stop being so stubborn. Unless they pay more attention, they're destined to be dunces. (Most frequently heard refrain from Teach: "Go and stand in the corner and don the pointy hat!")

Geminians are irritatingly intelligent and, although

they're not particularly brilliant at any one subject, they do OK. They *will* insist on getting up to mischief in class though. (Most frequently heard refrain from Teach: "Is it something you'd like to share with the rest of the class?")

Cancerians are quite good students but really need to swot to get good grades. They have to be in the right mood to concentrate though (when it's a New Moon preferably), and spend many a lesson staring blankly out of the window. (Most frequently heard refrain from Teach: "What *is* it that's so interesting out there?")

Leos love messing about. To a Leo, lessons are annoying interruptions to the one long lunch break that is their life. If they could be bothered to come in from the playground, they'd probably do quite well. (Most frequently heard refrain from Teach: "Didn't you hear the bell, cloth-ears?")

Virgoans insist on doing everything in their own inimitable style. They're popular with classmates, but teachers can't abide their Norman Know-it-all ways. (Most frequently heard refrain from Teach: "Put your hand down and let someone else answer!")

Librans think school is a right laugh. It's where they conduct their social life. They're not so keen on the lessons though. The teachers spoil things a bit too. And as for rules – well they're fun to break, but that's all. (Most frequently heard refrain from Teach: "Could you *please* turn off that mobile phone?!")

SEPTEMBER FORECAST

1st–7th

A tense aspect between the Sun and your ruler Pluto indicates a power struggle. You may feel like trampling down the opposition but you know in your heart that this won't make you popular. Don't let someone ride roughshod over your feelings either. Compromise is the keyword this week and it's vital that you reach one if you don't want this whole episode to end in tears.

Love:  ***Friends:***  ***Social life:*** 

8th–14th

A transiting Mercury means you refuse to believe anything unless you hear it straight from the horse's mouth. Gossip is of no interest to you: there are far more important things to think about right now – like yourself!

Love:  ***Friends:***  ***Social life:*** 

15th–21st

As Mars changes signs, beware of jealousy and steer clear of anyone you feel intuitively unsure of. Work goes well: after a tough time, expect to be top of the class this week! If you're taking any tests or exams, you'll do especially well. Entering competitions is well-starred too, so give that a try if you can squeeze it in between all the school work!

Love:  ***Friends:***  ***Social life:*** 

See page 176 for key to symbols

22nd–30th

With Mercury joining Venus in your sign this week, you're in a hyper-sociable mood. Spend as much time as you can with people you love, but try not to neglect your school work. People are queueing up to be your mate and you're the first name on everybody's party list.

Love:  ***Friends:***  ***Social life:*** 

OCTOBER 2000

Halloween Horrors

Use your psychic powers (and, yes, we all have them!), and this year's Halloween will be extra spooky!

Note: if any of the technical terms (in italics) used below baffle you, check the glossary on page 213.

As a **Scorpian**, you are fascinated by all things mysterious and this includes the world of psychic powers. With your amazing eyes and soft voice, you'd make a top hypnotist. Move over, Paul McKenna, and let Miss Scorpio take the stage!

Sagittarians are very open-minded and this can make them psychic in the most dramatic way. Many are *psychokinetic* and some even experience visions. If a Saggie were to choose a psychic career, they'd make a great prophet. (Well, *someone* has to do it . . !)

Capricornians, although quite cynical about psychic

See page 176 for key to symbols

stuff, are very tolerant and would never dismiss it as a load of twaddle. What they don't realize is that they're actually pretty psychic; they just don't pay too much attention to that part of themselves, that's all. A career as a colour therapist would suit a Capricorn – it's not too spooky but good intuition is vital. Something they have by the barrowload.

Aquarians are extremely positive and sensitive people and are able to pick up all sorts of signs and signals that others would miss completely. They're interested in what makes other folk tick and would do well studying *biorhythms.* In fact, they could even make a career of it if they wanted . . .

Pisceans are the dreamers of the zodiac. And that's why so many solutions, ideas and messages come to them whilst they're in the dream state. They're also pretty clairvoyant and are the most likely sign to see a ghost or apparition. If they fancied doing something spooky for a living, a Piscean would make a fab *medium.* (Just so long as they don't frighten themselves . . . they're easily spooked!)

Ariens have really good natural instincts: if they get a gut feeling about something, they're usually right. If they want to develop their psychic powers, they should concentrate on seeing into the future. They're also interested in *runes* and *phrenology.* If they were a psychic by trade, they'd be a fortune-teller.

Taureans, like Ariens, should also trust their instincts. Their hidden psychic ability is also *divination,* and they should concentrate on *numerology* and *dowsing* if they want to develop this talent. If they were to choose a psychic career, they'd be *numerologists.*

Geminians are naturally very crafty and clever and can often fool people into believing they're psychic. In actual fact, they are pretty *telepathic* and should use this power wisely. Other areas that may fascinate them are *palmistry* and *graphology.*

Cancerians are highly sensitive and this is a bonus if they're considering developing any psychic talents they might have. If they read up on tea leaf reading and *scrying,* they'd find it very interesting. Their secret psychic talents are *clairaudience* and *clairvoyance.*

Leos have a natural ability to connect with people. They're good with others on a one-to-one, face-to-face level and have a real interest in other people's lives. They sometimes have great powers of *precognition,* which can be useful. But it's astrology and tarot reading that really enthral a Leo.

Virgoans have extremely sharp intuition, but are rather dubious about the existence of psychic powers. They may not know this, but they actually have a powerful healing touch and would make excellent psychic healers. Next time someone close to them is feeling poorly, they should lay their hands on them and see what happens . . .

Librans are very understanding types and are psychically highly sensitive. Of all the signs, they're the one most likely to possess the ability to see *auras.* If they wanted a psychic career, one as an aura reader would suit them well.

Glossary

Aura = the subtle power that emanates from the body
Biorhythms = body "moods"
Clairaudience = "hearing" voices and/or sounds not perceptible to the other senses
Clairvoyance = the power of seeing or perceiving objects not perceptible to the other senses
Divination = the ability to see into the future
Dowsing = using a divining rod to discover underground water and/or minerals
Graphology = character analysis using handwriting
Medium = someone who can receive information from the "spirit world"
Numerologist = someone who studies the psychic significance of numbers
Numerology = the study of the significance of numbers
Palmistry = studying the hands and palms for character-reading and fortune-telling
Phrenology = character analysis using the bumps on the head!
Precognition = having visions of the future through dreams, ideas, feelings or visions
Psychokinetic = able to move objects without touching them
Runes = carved Scandinavian stones used for fortune-telling
Scrying = crystal ball reading
Telepathic = able to pick up and transmit thoughts without using the senses of sight, smell, hearing, taste or touch

OCTOBER FORECAST

1st–7th

You start the week with the Moon in your sign, which makes you rather sensitive – not so much to other people's feelings, just to your own. Avoid heavy discussions this week – you just won't be able to see things from someone else's point of view.

Love:  ***Friends:***  ***Social life:*** 

8th–14th

The Full Moon in the work part of your chart indicates big changes at school. You may feel happy about this at first, but the planets advise you not to complain too much and just go with the flow. You'll realize why all that's happening now is a good thing in a few weeks' time.

Love:  ***Friends:***  ***Social life:*** 

15th–21st

As Saturn moves backwards into your opposite sign, you could face a romantic dilemma. Why are you so scared of saying what (or who) you really want? Doing things because you feel you should isn't helping you or anyone else. So be honest, speak out and be happy!

Love:  ***Friends:***  ***Social life:*** 

22nd–31st

As the Sun enters Scorpio, you're feeling utterly fab. The new love in your life helps of course, but you'd be feeling confident even without this influence. You're the girl everyone wants to hang out with and you're looking gorgeous too! What an excellent time you're

See page 176 for key to symbols

going to have! (Even better if it's your birthday or if you have a Halloween party to attend!)

Love:  ***Friends:***  ***Social life:*** 

NOVEMBER 2000

Will Your Bonfire Night Go With A Bang?

The only good thing about the dreary month of November is Bonfire Night. Totally agree? Then you must be a Scorpian . . .

A true **Scorpian** such as yourself really enjoys bonfire parties – the fireworks, the weather and the fact that it's so close to your birthday sets you a-glow with excitement. It can make you feel rather sexy too and more likely than the other signs to cop off with someone.

Sagittarians, as Fire signs, love Guy Fawkes Night. They love parties even more, so the combination of the two is fab! They love getting involved with the setting off of fireworks, but, if there are any sensible people about, Saggies may not be allowed to get their hands on anything dangerous. (They're famous for their carelessness.)

Capricornians reckon that fireworks are dangerous and expensive and, because of this, they're unlikely to ever throw a Bonfire Night party of their own. They may attend someone else's party, but they'll stand well clear

See page 176 for key to symbols

of the fireworks and make a lot of tutting noises – much to everyone else's annoyance.

Aquarians think fireworks are an evil waste of money and believe that the cash spent on them every year should be used to buy far more worthy things. They're not overly keen on parties either, so probably wouldn't enjoy a bonfire do too much.

Pisceans hate noise and crowds: their idea of a nightmare would be a huge public fireworks display. A small party in someone's garden is bad enough, but they'll go if there's a free Lucozade to be had.

Ariens are a Fire signs and love a good Bonfire Night. Being ruled by Mars, they're the most likely sign to get burnt (metaphorically or physically) at a bonfire do, so they should be extra vigilant at all times and avoid lighting fireworks. They also get impatient with all the hanging around, and if a party's not well organized enough, they may start complaining. Or take over . . .

Taureans quite like Bonfire Night but aren't the biggest socializers in the zodiac. At a fireworks party, Taureans are invariably stood in the shadows, quietly scoffing baked potatoes. Copping off is a rare occurrence: their mouth's too full of grub to snog!!

Geminians *pretend* to like fireworks because fireworks look so cool, but deep down they're petrified of all the whizzing and banging. That's why they always find someone to snog at bonfire parties – they're much happier on a comfy sofa than in a chilly back yard!

Cancerians are always happy to help out at any sort of party, but those of the bonfire variety aren't really their favourites. They prefer edible bangers to the exploding kind and may just turn up for the scoff. And why not indeed . . . ?

Leos, as Fire signs, enjoy a good firework display. They're more inclined to attend a big public show than a house party, because they like their fireworks on a grand scale. At-home bonfire "do's" always seem to disappoint them – more so if there's not enough decent totty around . . .

Virgoans are sticklers for everything being just so, so the mess of a bonfire party can really upset them. Whether the party is their own or someone else's, a Virgoan is the "helpful" person hoovering the carpet and sweeping the patio – and, basically, not having very much fun at all.

Librans love the pretty colours of the fireworks and the whole atmosphere of a cracking bonfire party. But, because of the responsibility involved, they're unlikely to throw a party of their own. So they'll just go to other people's and have fun at their expense instead.

NOVEMBER FORECAST

1st–7th

A transiting Mars warns you of jealousy and resentment. Look at your closest relationships and ask yourself exactly what's going on? Could your nearest and dearest have it in for you in some way? Seems so.

Get to the root of the problem before Bonfire Night or the fireworks may not be of the variety you expect . . .

Love:  ***Friends:***  ***Social life:*** 

8th–14th

The Full Moon in your opposite sign marks a change in your love life: it seems you both want each other, but something (or someone) is getting in the way. Try to be patient – a solution is about to be found . . .

Love:  ***Friends:***  ***Social life:*** 

15th–21st

With the Sun entering the money part of your chart this week, there's no avoiding facing up to cash matters. You're in a positive mood, so try to cash in on your talents. Writing could prove profitable. Trouble is, you're easily distracted and may miss out on really obvious opportunities. Keep your eyes open and your ear to the ground if you want to feed your piggy-bank this week!

Love:  ***Friends:***  ***Social life:*** 

22nd–30th

The New Moon marks the start of a prosperous phase. It's a good time to make money, open a savings account or get your finances sorted. (You might as well – what *else* is there to do in the last dreary days of November?)

See page 176 for key to symbols

Love:  *Friends:*  *Social life:* 

DECEMBER 2000

Cosmic Christmas Gifts

Because, astrologically speaking, the outer and inner self are often totally different, what we want and what we actually get for Christmas are equally different. If you're wondering what gifts to buy your friends and family this year, read this first . . .

Every **Scorpian** (you included) is totally fed up with all the black tights and socks people throw their way every Christmas. It's not that you don't use them, it's just that you're now the proud owner of at least 150 pairs! Mates should make an effort to cheer you up this year by buying you some nice pink ones instead. It's this year's black anyway (maybe . . .)!

Sagittarians are always given outdoory, sporty clothes as pressies. Football shirts, anything in their fave teams' colours and big woolly jumpers. But all they really want is a bit of '70s glam. So go to town (steering well clear of Millets of course) and bring 'em back a glittery acrylic cardi and a pair of crimplene hot pants!

Capricornians, notorious for their dislike of extravagance, are always "treated" to cheap 'n'

See page 176 for key to symbols

cheerful gifts – shoelaces, a nice egg cup, a manicure set . . . Secretly though, they'd rather have something hideously expensive: in fact, anything that costs less than £1000, as far as they're concerned, is barely worth a thank-you note.

Aquarians, outwardly sane but inwardly mad as hatters, are often disappointed to find clothing made of tweed, itchy wool and corduroy in their Christmas stocking. If only people realized how much happier they'd be with some glittery nail polish, false eyelashes and an "I'm With Stupid" T-shirt!

Pisceans always get very elegant presents: perfume, original 1940s negligees and silk scarves mainly. But, unbeknown to many, they're actually pretty gauche and would be much happier with a pair of silly sunglasses and a weird wig. (Oh, and don't forget the funny fart cushion!)

Ariens are secretly rather glam, but because very few people actually realize this, they're likely to get something very practical for Christmas. They wish their friends and family would stop buying them sensible slippers and handy tool kits, and would splash out on some gorgeously sexy and frivolous undies instead.

Taureans are viewed as couldn't-care-less types, so people rarely put much thought into gifts for them. But Taureans are actually quite snooty, so anything cheap 'n' nasty *won't* be well received. In fact, the average Taurean would rather have nothing than something that isn't of the highest quality. So there you have it . . . Nothing it is!

Geminians, although cutely kitsch on the surface, are actually – on the sneak – a bit of a class act. They'd be eternally grateful for a nice pair of suede gloves. But what do they get? Fluffy mules and a feather boa – that's what! Ta very much, Santa . . .

Cancerians are modest types who don't ask for much. Yeah – right! Like they'd be happy with a set of hankies or a nice book! Forget it! Underneath that "no-really-I-just-don't-need-anything" exterior, lies a total pressie-grabber – the more the merrier as far as they're concerned.

Leos love very expensive, quality gifts. Simple, eh? So why does everyone insist on buying them such a load of old tack every Christmas? All they want is a nice little something in white gold or platinum, but no. Mates and Santa alike come bearing gifts of the see-thru' nightie, nasty perfume and cheap chocs variety instead.

Virgoans may seem shy, but beneath that slightly inhibited surface lies a complete wild child. Ask a Virgoan what they really want for Christmas and you may well be shocked by their answer. But a gnome hat and matching scarf is about as shocking as the pressies ever get. Sad but true . . .

Librans, although quite fluffy on the surface, would love nothing more than a nice pair of thermal longjohns. So why do friends and relatives shower them with exotic lingerie year in year out? OK, so they may look fab in a satin g-string, but they'd much rather have something for everyday wear.

DECEMBER FORECAST

1st–7th

Mercury leaves your sign and leaves you feeling more settled. Keep an eye on your money though, and don't lend or give a penny to anyone, no matter how convincing a sob story they give you!

Love: ***Friends:*** ***Social life:***

8th–14th

The Full Moon in your opposite sign means that a close relationship – with your best mate or boyfriend – hits a rocky patch. In fact, it could well have run its course. If you know this to be true, don't hang on. It's over – accept it. And don't get too distressed – someone else will soon come along and fill the gap.

Love: ***Friends:*** ***Social life:***

15th–21st

As the Sun prepares to change signs, you're full of enthusiasm and confidence. You'll shine most at pre-Xmas parties so get to as many as you can. A positive aspect between Venus and your ruling planet Pluto has you gagging for festive romance. Choose your new

See page 176 for key to symbols

paramour for his personality – not his looks – and you'll be on the right track. A Xmas party will lead to love – or at the very least an intense, passionate and emotional fling!

Love:  ***Friends:***  ***Social life:*** 

22nd–31st

Mercury in the communications part of your chart provides you with brilliant insight and great wit. If you need to impress anyone, you'll do it ten times over this week. In fact, you even impress *yourself* with your eloquence and charm! Mars in Scorpio from Xmas Eve gives you a whole load of energy. Make sure you get out and about – and use your energy wisely. If you don't, you could come down with a nasty bug or even have an accident. This Mars transit advises you to be especially wary of all hot and sharp objects: so avoid carving the turkey this year! With the New Moon in the communications part of your chart on Christmas Day, you can't fail to impress everyone. All pressies will be gratefully received; parties are well-starred; and you're feeling daring enough to go your own way and not go along with everyone else. What a girl!

Love:  ***Friends:***  ***Social life:*** 

See page 176 for key to symbols

Part 11:

Into The New Millennium!

What does the first part of the new millennium hold for you? How are you and your life going to change in the next decade? To find out the answers to these and a whole load more questions, check out our Ten-Year Forecast . . .

Growing Up And Branching Out

2001

The eclipse in January means serious changes to your future plans. You could begin to realize that you have to look further than your own back yard if you want to make your mark on the world. Jupiter starts moving forwards again on January 25th and this boosts your luck.

The eclipse in June forecasts more changes in your plans for the future: it seems that changing track completely may be the only way to go . . . Pluto changing direction in August improves your cash-flow situation no end. You must be honest though: any cash gained through dishonesty will soon be lost. Saturn going backwards from the end of September forecasts a sudden lack of blokes on the horizon. If you're looking for love, you may have to wait.

Neptune going forwards again in October sees you hanging onto the past. This won't do you any good, so concentrate on the here and now. From the end of October and throughout November, Uranus causes you to look for a new direction in life. You end the year with a passionate romance, but remember – there's a thin line between love and hate and around New Year's Eve you could be discovering just how true that old saying is . . .

A Restless Year 2002

Saturn changes direction in February and this helps you develop a more open-minded attitude towards certain close relationships. About time . . .

With Pluto following a similar pattern to last year, your finances could be a bit rollercoaster-y between March and August. With lusty Mars in the passion part of your chart from April 14th, your love life's pretty intense. That's not to say it'll be easy . . . Co-operation – sometimes tricky for a single-minded Scorpian – and compromise are the answers.

In October, Mars warns you that there's much jealousy and resentment around you. Make an effort to avoid people who are masquerading as mates, but who are really nothing of the sort. A retrograde Saturn in October forecasts a crisis in a close friendship or romance. Why are you feeling so guilty all the time? Make an effort to say what you want and the relationship should improve.

You're feeling restless but very much a party animal throughout November.

December's eclipse coincides with a loss of cash. Shouldn't spend so much on the Christmas pressies then, eh?

Life In The Fast Lane

2003

As energetic Mars leaves your sign on the 17th, you'll have some excellent money-making ideas. In March, Mars enters the communications part of your chart and you start to experience life in the fast lane. Around the same time, unpredictable planet Uranus changes signs and sees you looking for fun and romance. Whatever happens – this whole phase is enlightening and enjoyable.

May's eclipse in Scorpio sees you making an effort to chuck out all the stuff that doesn't matter to you any more. This could involve a wardrobe clear-out or could mean you'll be sorting the wheat from the chaff on the mates front.

Saturn changes signs in June, and helps you realize that you have to break free of all the stuff that's holding you back, and be more open-minded about your capabilities. You're in for a lusty time in July – it's not just the weather that'll be hot, hot hot!

A retrograde Saturn makes October a tense time, and an eclipse in your opposite sign on the 9th of November advises you to face up to any problems you might be having with your most intimate relationship. It's no good pretending they don't exist: get to the root of the problem and sort 'em out once and for all.

Get Scribbling! 2004

As Mercury transits two signs in January, you're all over the place, scattering your energy here, there and everywhere. Writing is extremely well-starred between the 7th and 21st, so whatever comes out of your pen will be pure genius! Get scribbling!

In May, the eclipse in your sign means big changes in your personal life. It could be the end of an era with regards to one phase and you may find this quite alarming. However, the planets advise you not to fight the changes – go with the flow and it'll all turn out for the best in the long run.

As Mars and Jupiter change signs towards the end of September, you realize that someone's got it in for you. Avoid anyone you think might be jealous or envious of you or yours, and try not to do anything devious. Keeping a low profile will make you more popular than ever.

Neptune changes direction in October and this bodes well for your home life. You and your family should get together and do something that makes you feel as if you're making a real contribution to the world.

In November, you're feeling much more on top of things; as long as you're quick to put your ideas into action, you're destined for BIG success.

Lust On Legs! 2005

As January dawns, you should keep a tight rein on your spending. Spring will be a joy-filled, family-orientated time until June, when a transiting Mars means the start of even *more* changes, this time at home. Holidays are well-starred, with a holiday romance a strong possibility. April's eclipse makes it ultra-important for you to get to understand your needs, especially those related to your health. From the end of May and for most of June, love and fun are well-starred.

The planet of responsibility, Saturn, changes signs in July, making you extra ambitious and determined to get to the top. In September, Pluto changes direction and this bodes well for money matters. As Jupiter enters Scorpio in October, you enter a brilliant – and lucky – chapter of your life. Your expectations are high and you can even afford to take a risk or two. (Not very Scorpian at all!) During this period, you'll mature and grow. Watch out for physical expansion too – many Scorpians are destined to "fill out" a bit during this transit.

In December, Mars changes direction in your opposite sign and indicates arguments between you and someone you're very close to. But on the plus side, just before Christmas, you're lust on legs and can use your sexiness to get whatever (and whoever) you want!

A Bad Start But A Happy Ending

2006

Mars remains in the "secrets" part of your chart for the whole of March, making life a bit weird. Also in March, a retrograde Jupiter in your sign could cause problems: you're supposed to be maturing, not regressing, so why are you acting like a ten-year-old? To add to your woes, Venus enters the work part of your chart in May and makes it hard for you to get things done.

In June, a retrograde Uranus creates a dilemma in your love life; you want it to be fun; he wants to get serious. Mmm . . . Despite this, the summer hols get off to a good start, with the emphasis on getting out and about and a transiting Venus in July bodes well for work. Don't underestimate the power of your sex appeal this month – it could get you just what you've always wanted, and a whole lot more.

In October, as Mercury enters your sign, you're advised that the best way to solve problems of the romantic kind is through talking. Keeping you feelings bottled up, although seemingly a good idea initially, won't help you or your bloke ultimately. Luck is indicated in November, especially on the love front, but only if you make an effort to think BIG. In December, Mars in the money part of your chart bodes well for any money-making ideas you might have.

Crucial Decisions And a Great Opportunity

2007

Mars moves into the communications part of your chart in January, helping you to make crucial decisions that could alter your life quite radically. As 2007 begins, you seem to be putting most of your energies into coming up ideas and getting them across to others. In February, you're likely to be presented with a great opportunity. Take it while you can – it won't be on offer for ever . . .

The eclipse in March causes big changes on the friends front. If you're having trouble with one friend in particular in April, talk things through during the first week of the month. In May, Neptune changes direction in the domestic part of your chart: any big ideas you have regarding your home or family may have to be put on hold. In September, an old friend could give you some great advice. Take it!

Mars goes backwards in November and this means that although you want to take risks, you can't quite bring yourself to do it. This isn't really a problem though: as Uranus changes direction around the same time, you become distracted by a new love interest.

In December, Jupiter enters the communications part of your chart and helps you get out of a rut.

A Very Special Year

2008

Pluto, your ruler and the planet of transformation, last changed signs back in 1995, but now, as the New Year dawns, it's ready to move into your astrological house of communications. This means that the year 2008, from the 26th of January onwards, is destined to be a very special one for you. An idea you have and people you meet this year are destined to have a profound effect on your life and affect your general attitude and way of thinking.

From the end of May and for most of June, Venus and Mercury link love to travel. In June, Pluto starts moving backwards, causing you to feel very passionate about someone or something. Do NOT, under any circumstances, dismiss these feelings. The total eclipse in August indicates big changes at work, and some old relationships will alter as a result. In October, Mars in Scorpio gives you extra energy.

As Mars leaves your sign on November 16th, your attention turns to making money – your speciality! You become more attractive and this, along with the fact that Uranus changes direction at the beginning of December, sees you starting a new romance.

Christmas and New Year will be fun-filled and fabulous. Just the way they should be . . .

Broadening Your Horizons

2009

When Jupiter joins Mars in the home and family part of your chart on January 6th, there may be some upheaval going on at home – you could be swapping rooms with someone, or even moving house. Around the same time, money luck is forecast. With Pluto now settled for the whole of the year, you're ready to make some improvements, both to your life and to yourself. This could start with you thinking about using computers or other modern methods of communication to broaden your horizons. Writing may interest you and you could begin to look into this as a possible career. Venus makes June a really special time for you.

You're feeling hot in July – and that's not down to the weather! You're so sexy that you're totally irresistible. Use your charms wisely – there is such a thing as too many boyfriends, you know! This could be why August and September is such a row-filled time for you, especially with regards to your love life.

In October, Saturn changes signs, making you finally realize that being paranoid isn't getting you anywhere. By November, you're feeling a lot stronger. As Christmas approaches, you're in an outgoing and sociable frame of mind.

Older And Wiser

2010

Lucky Jupiter enters the love and fun part of your chart on January 18th and this could indicate a romantic interlude. In February, more fun is forecast, with parties and celebrations galore.

Mars changes direction in March and gives you the energy and initiative to get out of any trouble you may have got into at work. At the end of May, Uranus enters the work part of your chart and marks the start of a whole new phase of your life. Your attention turns to your career and you face up to stuff you haven't been brave enough to look at before. Your intuition sharpens throughout this period and certain psychic talents may even come to your notice. Saturn makes a transit in July: for three years it's been holding you back, but now it moves on, helping you concentrate on building up your confidence and self-esteem.

In August, you'll be having a whale of a time, meeting new mates and starting a new romantic relationship. Mars in your sign from September to October gives you the strength and determination to do well, and Venus in your sign in November makes for a pleasant and relaxing time. Venus puts you in a lovely mood over Christmas and New Year, making it a good time for parties, celebrations and visiting friends and relatives. At the end of the decade, one thing's for sure: you're not only ten years older than you were at the start – you're ten years wiser too!

Part 12:

Birthday Chart

Not sure which friend is which star sign? Need an at-a-glance reminder of all your mates' birthdays? Want to know which celeb shares your date of birth? Then fill in this specially devised (starting with Aries and ending with Pisces) birthday chart and fret no more . . .

ARIES

March

20

21 Mark Hamilton (Ash), 1977; Ario (N'Tyce), 1974

22

23 Damon Albarn (Blur), 1968; Marti Pellow, 1966

24

25 Elton John, 1947; Mel (All Saints), 1975

26

27 Mariah Carey, 1969

28

29 Coree (Damage), 1978

30 Celine Dion, 1968

31

April

1 Chris Evans and Jean Claude Van Damme, 1966; Phillip Schofield, 1962

2 Linford Christie, 1960

3 Will Mellor, 1976

4 Robert Downey Jnr, 1965

5

6 Chantal (N-Tyce), 1977

7 Victoria Adams, 1975

8

9

10

11 Cerys Matthews, 1966

12 Paul Nicholls, 1979

13

14

15

16

17

18

19

TAURUS

20 Luther Vandross, 1951

21 The Queen, 1926

22

23

24 Jas Mann (Babylon Zoo), 1971

25

26

27

28

29 Michelle Pfeiffer, 1958

30

May

1 Joanna Lumley, 1947

2

3 Jay Darlington (Kula Shaker), 1969

4

5

6

7

8 Dave Rowntree (Blur), 1964

9

10 Bono (U2), 1960

11 Harry Enfield, 1961

12 Emilio Estevez, 1962

13

14 Sinead (B*Witched), 1978; Nat (All Saints), 1973

15

16 Janet Jackson, 1966

17

18

19

20 Sean Conlon (5ive), 1981; Cher, 1946

GEMINI

21

22 Naomi Campbell, 1970

23

24

25

26 Lenny Kravitz, 1964

27 Paul Gascoigne, 1964; Denise Van Outen, 1974

28 Kylie Minogue, 1968

29 Adam Rickitt, 1978; Noel Gallagher, 1967; Mel B, 1975

30 Sally Whittaker (Coronation Street), 1963

31

June

1

2

3

4 Noah Wyle, 1971

5

6

7 Prince, 1958

8 Mick Hucknall, 1960

9 Johnny Depp, 1963; Michael J. Fox, 1961

10 Liz Hurley, 1965

11

12

13 Jason Brown (5ive), 1976

14 Boy George, 1961

15 Courtney Cox, 1967

16

17

18 Paul McCartney, 1942

19

20 Nicole Kidman, 1966

CANCER

21 Prince William, 1982

22

23

24

25 Jamie Redknapp, 1973; George Michael, 1963

26

27

28 Adam Woodyatt (Ian Beale in EastEnders), 1969

29 Richard Abindin Breen (5ive), 1979

30

July

1 Keith Duffy (Boyzone), 1974; Pamela Anderson, 1967

2

3 Shane Lynch (Boyzone), 1976; Tom Cruise, 1962

4

5

6 Sylvester Stallone, 1946

7

8

9 Tom Hanks, 1956

10 Neil Tennant (Pet Shop Boys), 1954

11 Richie Sambora (Bon Jovi), 1960

12 Anna Friel, 1976

13 Harrison Ford, 1947

14

15

16

17

18

19 Anthony Edwards (ER), 1962

20

21 Ross Kemp (EastEnders), 1964; Robin Williams, 1952

22

LEO

23

24

25 Matt Le Blanc, 1967

26

27

28

29

30 Sean Moore (Manic Street Preachers), 1970; Arnold Schwarzenegger, 1947

31 Fatboy Slim, 1963

August

1

2

3

4

5

6 Geri Halliwell, 1972; Barbara Windsor (Peggy in EastEnders), 1937

7 David Duchovny, 1960

8

9 Whitney Houston, 1963

10

11 Andrez (Damage), 1978

12

13

14 Halle Berry, 1968

15 Mikey Graham, 1972 (Boyzone); Spike (911), 1974

16 Madonna, 1958

17 Robert de Niro, 1943

18 Christian Slater, 1969; Patrick Swayze, 1952

19

20

21 Dina Carroll, 1968

22 Howard Dwayne Dorough (Backstreet Boys), 1973

VIRGO

23 Richard Neville (5ive), 1979; Shaun Ryder, 1962

24 Stephen Fry, 1957

25 Elvis Costello, 1958

26 Macaulay Culkin, 1980

27

28

29 Michael Jackson, 1958

30

31 Richard Gere, 1949

September

1 Gloria Estefan, 1957

2 Keanu Reeves, 1965

3 Charlie Sheen, 1965

4 Kevin Kennedy (Coronation Street), 1961

5

6

7

8

9 Hugh Grant, 1960

10

11

12
13
14
15
16
17
18
19 Jarvis Cocker, 1966; Paul Winterhart (Kula Shaker), 1971
20
21 Liam Gallagher, 1972; Jimmy Constable (911), 1973
22

LIBRA

23
24
25 Declan Donnelly, 1977; Will Smith, 1968
26
27 Lee Anthony Brennan (911), 1975
28
29 Brett Anderson (Suede), 1967
30

October

1
2 Sting, 1952
3 Kevin Scott Richardson (Backstreet Boys), 1972
4 Alicia Silverstone, 1976
5 Kate Winslet, 1975

6

7 Michelle (N-Tyce), 1974

8

9

10

11 Dawn French, 1957

12

13

14 Shaznay (All Saints), 1975; Cliff Richard, 1940

15

16

17

18

19

20 Dannii Minogue, 1970

21 Donna (N-Tyce), 1976

22 Jeff Goldblum, 1952; Zac Hanson, 1985

SCORPIO

23

24 Alonza Bevan (Kula Shaker), 1970

25

26

27

28 Joaquin Phoenix, 1977; Julia Roberts, 1967

29 Winona Ryder, 1971

30

31

November

1

2

3 Ras (Damage), 1976; Roseanne, 1952

4 Kavanna, 1977; Louise Nurding, 1974

5 Bryan Adams, 1959

6 Ethan Hawke, 1970

7

8

9

10

11 Leonardo DiCaprio, 1974; Demi Moore, 1962

12 David Schwimmer, 1966

13 Whoopi Goldberg, 1955

14 Prince Charles, 1948; Usher, 1978

15

16

17 Jonathan Ross, 1960; Ike Hanson, 1980

18 Ant McPartlin , 1975

19 Meg Ryan, 1961; Jodie Foster, 1962

20

21 Alex James (Blur), 1968

22 Scott Robinson (5ive), 1979

SAGITTARIUS

23 Zoe Ball, 1970

24

25

26 Tina Turner, 1939

27

28 Dane (Another Level), 1979

29 Ryan Giggs, 1973

30 Gary Lineker, 1960

December

1

2

3

4

5

6

7 Aaron Carter, 1987; Nic (All Saints), 1974

8 Kim Basinger, 1953; Sinead O'Connor, 1966

9

10

11

12

13

14 Michael Owen, 1979

15 Adele & Keavey (B*Witched), 1979

16

17

18 Lindsay (B*Witched), 1980; Brad Pitt, 1965; Robson Green, 1964; Stephen Spielberg, 1947

19

20

21 Jamie Theakston, 1970

CAPRICORN

22 Noel Edmonds, 1948

23

24

25

26 Jared Leto, 1969

27

28 Denzel Washington, 1954

29

30

31 Val Kilmer, 1959

January

1 Noel (Damage), 1976

2

3 Mel Gibson, 1956

4 Tim (Ash), 1977; Beth Gibbons (Portishead), 1965; Michael Stipe (REM), 1960

5

6 Rowan Atkinson, 1956

7

8 David Bowie, 1947; Karen Poole (Alisha's Attic), 1971

9 AJ (Backstreet Boys), 1978

10 Rod Stewart, 1945

11

12 Mel C, 1976

13

14

15

16 Kate Moss, 1974

17 Jim Carrey, 1962

18 Kevin Costner, 1955; Crispian Mills (Kula Shaker), 1973

19

20 Gary Barlow, 1971

AQUARIUS

21 Emma Bunton, 1976

22

23

24 Vic Reeves, 1959

25

26

27 Mark Owen, 1974

28 Nick Carter (Backstreet Boys), 1980; Elijah Wood, 1981

29

30

31

February

1

2

3

4 Natalie Imbruglia, 1975

5 Bobby Brown, 1969

6

7 Axl Rose (Guns 'n' Roses), 1962; Danny Goffey (Supergrass), 1974

8

9

10

11 Brandy (Jennifer Brandy Norwood), 1979

12 Jade Jones (Damage), 1979

13 Robbie Williams, 1974

14

15

16

17

18 Matt Dillon, 1964; John Travolta, 1954

PISCES

19

20 Ian Brown (Stone Roses), 1963; Cindy Crawford, 1966

21 James Bradfield (Manic Street Preachers), 1969

22

23 Drew Barrymore, 1975

24

25

26

27 Peter Andre, 1973

28

29

March

1

2 Jon Bon Jovi, 1962

3 Ronan Keating (Boyzone), 1977

4 Evan Dando, 1967; Patsy Kensit, 1968

5

6 Shaquille O'Neal, 1972

7

8

9

10 Neneh Cherry, 1964

11

12 Graham Coxon (Blur), 1969; Kelly Bryan (Eternal), 1975

13 Adam Clayton (U2), 1960

14 Taylor Hanson, 1983

15

16 Jimmy Nail, 1954

17 Stephen Gately (Boyzone), 1976

18

19 Bruce Willis, 1955